# BELTANE

*Llewellyn's Sabbat Essentials*

# BELTANE

*Rituals, Recipes & Lore for May Day*

Llewellyn Publications
Woodbury, Minnesota

FIRST EDITION
Ninth Printing, 2021

Book design: Donna Burch-Brown
Cover art: iStockphoto.com/5855301/©procurator, iStockphoto.com
        /18050233/©denzorro, iStockphoto.com/21200270/©jut13,
        iStockphoto.com/18232461/©Electric_Crayon
Cover design: Kevin R. Brown
Interior illustrations: Mickie Mueller

Llewellyn Publications is a registered trademark of Llewellyn Worldwide Ltd.

**Library of Congress Cataloging-in-Publication Data**
Marquis, Melanie, 1976–
  Beltane : rituals, recipes, and lore for May day / by Melanie Marquis. — First edition.
      pages cm. — (Llewellyn's sabbat essentials ; #2)
  Includes bibliographical references and index.
  ISBN 978-0-7387-4193-2
1. Beltane. 2. May Day. 3. Witchcraft. I. Title.
  BF1572.B44M37 2014
  299'.94—dc23                                  2014021887

Llewellyn Publications
A Division of Llewellyn Worldwide Ltd.
2143 Woodale Drive
Woodbury, MN 55125-2989
www.llewellyn.com
Printed in the United States of America

# Contents

...tection, purification, manifestation, handfastings, building sacred

visiting sacred wells, giving offerings, working with faeries, ritu...

...alking the boundaries of one's property, protecting plants, divin...

animals, people, and possessions astronomical midpoint, and sun...

...n the spring equinox and summer solstice: Sun at 15 degrees o...

in the northern hemisphere, Sun at 15 degrees of Scorpio in ...

...outhern hemisphere. Female: Maiden Goddess, Mother Godd...

...Earth Goddess, water plants or animals, the Lover prepari...

...e with her beloved Flora, Danu, Freyja, Maia, Shasti, Pro...

Chin-hua fu-jen, Venus, Diana, Artemis, Aphrodite, Astar...

Bona, Rauni, Sarasvati, Horae, Pan, Cernunnos, Beal, Bel...

Pluto Wotan, Odin, Oak King, Apollo, Ra, Mugwort S...

fertility, protection, divination, communication, with spirits ene...

purification, joy, love, prophetic dreams, renewal energy, vitalit...

wealth, fairy magick, luck success, strength Rose, Frankincens...

Jasmine, Lemon, Pine, Mint visiting sacred wells, giving off...

faeries, abundance, growth, passion, love, union, cooperation, ferti...

...tection, purification, manifestation, handfastings, building sacre...

# LLEWELLYN'S SABBAT ESSENTIALS

LLEWELLYN'S SABBAT ESSENTIALS provides instruction and inspiration for honoring each of the modern witch's sabbats. Packed with spells, rituals, meditations, history, lore, invocations, divination, recipes, crafts, and more, each book in this eight-volume series explores both the old and new ways of celebrating the seasonal rites that act as cornerstones in the witch's year.

There are eight sabbats, or holidays, celebrated by Wiccans and many other Neopagans (modern Pagans) today. Together, these eight sacred days make up what's known as the Wheel of the Year, or the sabbat cycle, with each sabbat corresponding to an important turning point in nature's annual journey through the seasons.

Devoting our attention to the Wheel of the Year allows us to better attune ourselves to the energetic cycles of nature and listen to what each season is whispering (or shouting!) to us, rather than working against the natural tides. What better time to start new projects than as the earth reawakens after a long winter, and suddenly everything is blooming and growing and shooting up out of the ground again? And what better time to meditate and plan ahead than during the introspective slumber of winter? With Llewellyn's Sabbat Essentials, you'll learn how to focus on the spiritual aspects of the Wheel of the Year, how to move through it and with it in harmony, and how to celebrate your own ongoing growth and achievements. This may be your first book on Wicca, Witchcraft, or Paganism, or your newest addition to a bookcase or e-reader already crammed with magical wisdom. In either case, we hope you will find something of value here to take with you on your journey.

## Take a Trip Through the Wheel of the Year

The eight sabbats each mark an important point in nature's annual cycles. They are depicted as eight evenly spaced spokes on a wheel representing the year as a whole; the dates on which they fall are nearly evenly spaced on the calendar, as well.

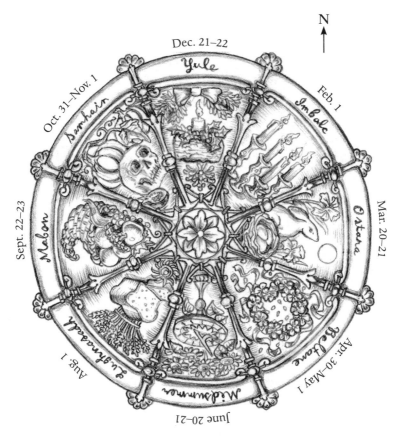

*Wheel of the Year—Northern Hemisphere*
*(All solstice and equinox dates are approximate,*
*and one should consult an almanac or a calendar*
*to find the correct dates each year.)*

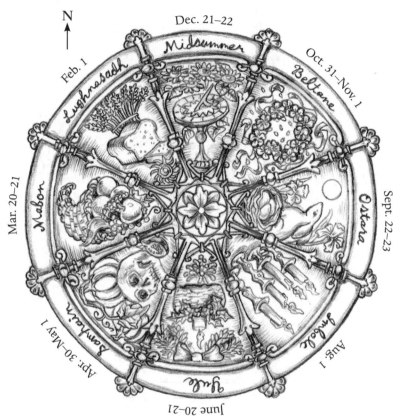

*Wheel of the Year—Southern Hemisphere*

The Wheel is comprised of two groups of four holidays each. There are four solar festivals relating to the sun's position in the sky, dividing the year into quarters: the Spring Equinox, the

Summer Solstice, the Fall Equinox, and the Winter Solstice, all of which are dated astronomically and thus vary slightly from year to year. Falling in between these quarter days are the cross-quarter holidays, or fire festivals: Imbolc, Beltane, Lughnasadh, and Samhain. The quarters are sometimes called the Lesser Sabbats and the cross-quarters the Greater Sabbats, although neither cycle is "superior" to the other. In the Southern Hemisphere, seasons are opposite those in the north, and the sabbats are consequently celebrated at different times.

While the book you are holding only focuses on Beltane, it can be helpful to know how it fits in with the cycle as a whole.

The Winter Solstice, also called Yule or Midwinter, occurs when nighttime has reached its maximum length; after the solstice, the length of the days will begin to increase. Though the cold darkness is upon us, there is a promise of brighter days to come. In Wiccan lore, this is the time when the young solar god is born. In some Neopagan traditions, this is when the Holly King is destined to lose the battle to his lighter aspect, the Oak King. Candles are lit, feasts are enjoyed, and evergreen foliage is brought in the house as a reminder that, despite the harshness of winter, light and life have endured.

At Imbolc (also spelled Imbolg), the ground is just starting to thaw, signaling that it's time to start preparing the fields for the approaching sowing season. We begin to awaken from our months of introspection and start to sort out what we have learned over that time, while also taking the first steps to make plans for our future. Some Wiccans also bless candles at Imbolc, another symbolic way of coaxing along the now perceptibly stronger light.

On the Spring Equinox, also known as Ostara, night and day are again equal in length, and following this, the days will grow longer than the nights. The Spring Equinox is a time of renewal, a time to plant seeds as the earth once again comes to life. We decorate eggs as a symbol of hope, life, and fertility, and we perform rituals to energize ourselves so that we can find the power and passion to live and grow.

In agricultural societies, Beltane marked the start of the summer season. Livestock were led out to graze in abundant pastures and trees burst into beautiful and fragrant blossom. Rituals were performed to protect crops, livestock, and people. Fires were lit and offerings were made in the hopes of gaining divine protection. In Wiccan mythos, the young goddess is impregnated by the young god. We all have something we want to harvest by the end of the year—plans we are determined to realize—and Beltane is a great time to enthusiastically get that process in full swing.

The Summer Solstice is the longest day of the year. It's also called Litha or Midsummer. Solar energies are at their apex, and the power of Nature is at its height. In Wiccan lore, it's the time when the solar god's power is at its greatest (so, paradoxically, his power must now start to decrease), having impregnated the maiden goddess, who then transforms into the earth mother. In some Neopagan traditions, this is when the Holly King once again battles his lighter aspect, this time vanquishing the Oak King. It's generally a time of great merriment and celebration.

At Lughnasadh, the major harvest of the summer has ripened. Celebrations are held, games are played, gratitude is expressed, and feasts are enjoyed. Also known as Lammas, this is the time we celebrate the first harvest—whether that means the first of our garden crops or the first of our plans that have come to fruition. To celebrate the grain harvest, bread is often baked on this day.

The Autumn Equinox, also called Mabon, marks another important seasonal change and a second harvest. The sun shines equally on both hemispheres, and the lengths of night and day are equal. After this point, the nights will again be longer than the days. In connection with the harvest, the day is celebrated as a festival of sacrifice and of the dying god, and tribute is paid to the sun and the fertile earth.

To the Celtic people, Samhain marked the start of the winter season. It was the time when the livestock was slaughtered and the final harvest was gathered before the inevitable plunge into the depths of winter's darkness. Fires were lit to help wandering spirits on their way, and offerings were given in the names of the gods and the ancestors. Seen as a beginning, Samhain is now often called the Witches' New Year. We honor our ancestors, wind down our activities, and get ready for the months of introspection ahead … and the cycle continues.

## The Modern Pagan's Relationship to the Wheel

Modern Pagans take inspiration from many pre-Christian spiritual traditions, exemplified by the Wheel of the Year. The cycle of eight festivals we recognize throughout modern Pagandom today was never celebrated in full by any one particular pre-Christian culture. In the 1940s and 1950s a British man named Gerald Gardner created the new religion of Wicca by drawing on a variety of cultures and traditions, deriving and adapting practices from pre-Christian religion, animistic beliefs, folk magick, and various shamanic disciplines and esoteric orders. He combined multicultural equinox and solstice traditions with Celtic feast days and early European agricultural and pastoral celebrations to create a single model that became the framework for the Wiccan ritual year.

This Wiccan ritual year is popularly followed by Wiccans and witches, as well as many eclectic Pagans of various stripes. Some Pagans only observe half of the sabbats, either the quarters or the cross-quarters. Other Pagans reject the Wheel of the Year altogether and follow a festival calendar based on the culture of whatever specific path they follow rather than a nature-based agrarian cycle. We all have such unique paths in Paganism that it is important not to make any assumptions about another's based on your own; maintaining an open and positive attitude is what makes the Pagan community thrive.

Many Pagans localize the Wheel of the Year to their own environment. Wicca has grown to become a truly global religion, but few of us live in a climate mirroring Wicca's British Isles origins. While traditionally Imbolc is the beginning of the thaw and the awakening of the earth, it is the height of winter in many northern climes. While Lammas may be a grateful celebration of the harvest for some, in areas prone to drought and forest fires it is a dangerous and uncertain time of year.

There are also the two hemispheres to consider. While it's winter in the Northern Hemisphere, it's summer in the Southern Hemisphere. While Pagans in America are celebrating Yule and the Winter Solstice, Pagans in Australia are celebrating Midsummer. The practitioner's own lived experiences are more important than any dogma written in a book when it comes to observing the sabbats.

In that spirit, you may wish to delay or move up celebrations so that the seasonal correspondences better fit your own locale, or you may emphasize different themes for each sabbat as you experience it. This series should make such options easily accessible to you.

No matter what kind of place you live on the globe, be it urban, rural, or suburban, you can adapt sabbat traditions and practices to suit your own life and environment. Nature is all around us; no matter how hard we humans try to insulate ourselves from nature's cycles, these recurring seasonal changes are inescapable. Instead of swimming against the tide, many modern Pagans embrace each season's unique energies, whether dark, light, or in-between, and integrate these energies into aspects of our own everyday lives.

Llewellyn's Sabbat Essentials offer all the information you need in order to do just that. Each book will resemble the one you hold in your hands. The first chapter, *Old Ways*, shares the history and lore that have been passed down, from mythology and pre-Christian traditions to any vestiges still seen in modern life. *New Ways* then spins those themes and elements into the manners in which modern Pagans observe and celebrate the sabbat. The next chapter focuses on *Spells and Divination* appropriate to the season or based in folklore, while the following one, *Recipes and Crafts*, offers ideas for decorating your home, hands-on crafts, and recipes that take advantage of seasonal offerings. The chapter on *Invocations and Meditations* provides ready-made calls and prayers you may use in ritual, meditation, or journaling. The *Rituals and Celebrations* chapter provides three complete rituals: one for a solitary, one for two people, and one for a whole group such as a coven, circle, or grove. (Feel free to adapt each or any ritual to your own needs, substituting your own offerings, calls, invocations, magical workings, and so on. When planning a group ritual, try to be conscious of any special needs participants may have. There are many wonderful books available that delve into the fine points of facilitating ritual if you don't have experience in this department.) Finally, in the back of the book you'll find a complete list of correspondences for the holiday, from magical themes to deities to foods, colors, symbols, and more.

By the end of this book you'll have the knowledge and the inspiration to celebrate the sabbat with gusto. By honoring the Wheel of the Year, we reaffirm our connection to nature so that as her endless cycles turn, we're able to go with the flow and enjoy the ride.

OLD WAYS

...ance, growth, passion, love, union, cooperation, fertility party...
...ction, purification, manifestation, handfastings, building sacred...
...isiting sacred wells, giving offerings, working with faeries, vitali...
...lking the boundaries of one's property, protecting plants, divina...
...imals, people, and possessions astronomical midpoint, and summ...
...the spring equinox and summer solstice. Sun at 15 degrees of...
...the northern hemisphere, Sun at 15 degrees of Scorpio in th...
...thern hemisphere. Female: Maiden Goddess, Mother Godde...
...Earth Goddess, water plants or animals, the Lover preparing...
...with her beloved Flora, Danu, Freya, Maia, Shasti, Prosp...
...hin-hua fu-jen, Venus, Diana, Artemis, Aphrodite, Astarte,...
...na, Raeni, Sarasvati, Horae, Pan, Cernunnos, Beal, Baldu...
...Pluto Wotan, Odin, Oak King, Apollo, Ra, Mugwort Zeus...
...rtility, protection, divination, communication, with spirits energy...
...urification, joy, love, prophetic dreams, renewal energy, vitality,...
...ealth, fairy magick, luck success, strength Rose, Frankincense,...
...smine, Lemon, Pine, Mint visiting sacred wells, giving offere...
...nces, abundance, growth, passion, love, union, cooperation, fertile...
...ction, purification, manifestation, handfastings, building sacred...

*I*N THIS CHAPTER, we'll explore some of the history and lore surrounding Beltane, so that you'll have a deeper well of inspiration with which to satisfy the thirst of your own creativity and spirit of innovation. We magickal folks have always honored tradition while at the same time adapting those traditions to better reflect our own experience with the natural world around us. As you'll see, Beltane has been honored in many different ways each unique to its own time and place, yet common themes of growth, protection, abundance, fertility, light, love, and sexuality can be found throughout.

Beltane is the cross-quarter day falling roughly halfway between the Spring Equinox and the Summer Solstice—a time when days are growing longer and the sun's strength is waxing. It's six months after Samhain, another of the cross-quarter holidays. Beltane is a time when flowers begin to bloom and green plants enjoy a growth spurt. It's a time of fertility and growth; a time to celebrate love, light, and sexuality.

In Wiccan metaphor, Beltane can be seen as the time when the solar earth deity, or Horned God, has grown up into a lusty young man ready to mate with the lunar earth goddess, or Triple Goddess, in her youthful, sensual maiden aspect, ripe for fertilizing. It can be seen as the time of year when the Oak King, symbolic of the earth god's lighter half, reigns supreme, having triumphed over his twin, rival, and darker side, the Holly King, at the preceding winter solstice. The Holly King and Oak King are not originally Celtic ideas, as they are often erroneously attributed; rather, these archetypes were first popularized in Robert Graves's book *The White Goddess*, and can be understood as representations of the timeless myth of the annual battle between winter and summer, dark and light, that we find in many cultures (Bramshaw, 222). According to Graves, while the Holly King rules the darker, waning half of the year, a time when the sun is fading and days are growing shorter, the Oak King presides over the waxing, lighter, brighter half of the year.

Beltane celebrations are most commonly held beginning at sundown on April 30 and ending at sundown on May 1 (October 31 through November 1 in the Southern Hemisphere). There are, however, other ways to time the festival. You might time it to fall *exactly* between the Spring Equinox and the Summer Solstice, in which case, if you're a Northern Hemisphere witch, you would hold your celebration when the ecliptic longitude of the sun reaches 45 degrees. You might determine the date by observing signs in nature. In Celtic lands, the hawthorn trees were generally in their flowering stage when the proper time for the festival arrived; you might decide to celebrate Beltane when the hawthorns or other flowering thorn trees in your area burst into bloom. The Celtic festival of Beltaine corresponded with the time when livestock were moved into summer pastures to graze; if you're a livestock farmer, you might choose to plan your own Beltane celebration to sync up in the same way.

You might, like some Druids of the past and the present, determine the proper date by following the movement of the stars. You could time your celebration to coincide with the point where the sun is positioned at 15 degrees relative to Taurus. Taurus, symbolized by the bull, is one of the four fixed cardinal signs of the zodiac and an important "power point" in the astrological year. The Druids, according to Julius Caesar, placed great importance on learning about "the stars and their movements," (Littleton) and their positioning in relation to the earth and the sun was likely believed to have influence over the everyday lives of humans, connecting people to Nature's ever-changing energetic currents. With Taurus the bull as its astrological ruler, Beltane brings with it energies capable of renewing life and enhancing growth. It's a time of increasing strength, a time of vitality, a time of fertility and sexuality. It's a time to connect to the living, breathing energies of the universe, a time to give thanks, and a time to ask for continued blessings and to secure supernatural protections. Ultimately, Beltane is a time to thrive and grow.

Beltane, as we modern Pagans know it, has its roots in the ancient Roman festival of Floralia as well as in the early Pre-Christian Celtic festival of Beltaine and other European May Day celebrations. Our modern Beltane is a composite of many different traditions, a blending of cultures, beliefs, and customs reflecting a common urge to welcome the coming of May and the warmer temperatures and thriving vegetation that comes with it.

Our modern Neopagan Beltane borrows its name and some of its more prominent customs from the early Pre-Christian Celtic festival of Beltaine, which celebrated the midpoint of the Celtic year and the beginning of the summer season. A pastoral people, the early Celts understood the year as twofold: there was the darker, colder half of the year beginning at Samhain that coincided with the time when cattle were slaughtered, and there was the lighter, warmer half of the year beginning at Beltaine that marked the time when cattle were led out to open summer pastures to graze.

Beltaine was celebrated in Ireland, Scotland, and the Isle of Man, and many of its customs were adopted in other areas of Great Britain and Europe. The festival was known as *Bealtaine* to the Irish and *Bealltainn* in Scottish Gaelic, both names derived from a common Celtic word meaning "bright fire."

The festival of Beltaine may have been originally connected to the worship of the Celtic god Belenus. Belenus was a widely recognized deity associated with healing, and his worship dates all the way back to prehistoric times (Jordan, 48). While Belenus is closely related to the Roman Apollo, a god of light and the sun, in Celtic culture Belenus was associated with fountains, health, and the pastoral lifestyle. Belenus is associated with the symbols of the phallic shaped stone, the bull, the horse, and the oak. As one of the Celtic high gods, Belenus was known in Ireland, Scotland, Wales, France, Italy, Spain, England, and elsewhere. He was alternatively named Belen, Belenos, Belinus, Bellinus, Bélénos, Belennos, Bel, and other monikers, according to place, language, and tradition. Inscriptions to Belenus are found at many sites, primarily in France and Italy, but in other places in Europe as well. Inscriptions to Belenus have even been found in North America. At a site in New Hampshire called Mystery Hill, a 30-acre complex believed to have been a ritual site for early European explorers, among the findings was a stone tablet bearing an Ogham inscription that translates as "Dedicated to Bel" (Angel; Fleming).

While there is very little historical record and even less archeological evidence that illuminates much detail about early Celtic Beltaine rituals, we can surmise that these rituals were primarily focused on protecting cattle, crops, dairy products, and people and on encouraging fertility and growth. While Samhain was a time to connect with darker energies, Beltaine was a time to tune in to the current of life, renewal, and optimism.

Fire seems to have played a big role in Beltaine ceremonies. The earliest mention of the festival of Beltaine is found in an early medieval text from Ireland written by Cormac, bishop of Cashel and king of Munster. The text reports a festival held May 1 to mark the beginning of summer, and it describes a fire ritual performed at this time by the Druids. Two fires were made, and as incantations were spoken, cattle were forced to pass between the two torrents of raging flames. Another early mention of Beltaine comes from the seventeenth century historian Geoffrey Keating, who describes a huge gathering on the Hill of Uisneach in Ireland involving two bonfires, a stream of cattle passing between the flames, and a sacrifice made to a god named Bel. These actions were believed to protect the cattle from disease and thus safeguard the supply of dairy products and meat that were important supplements to the Celts' diet (Hyde, 90).

Household fires were extinguished at Beltaine, then re-lit from communal bonfires. Both cattle and people walked between two raging bonfires or, alternatively, walked a circuit around the fire or jumped over the leaping flames as a magickal act intended to ensure a good harvest.

We know much more about Beltaine customs practiced in the late eighteenth century onward, as such traditions eventually gained the interest of folklorists who thought it prudent to take record of the continuations of this long-surviving Pagan rite. Many Beltaine customs remained relatively unchanged over the centuries. Beltaine bonfires retained popularity, and throughout the nineteenth century, the practice of driving cattle between two bonfires to ensure their health and protection was common throughout many parts of Ireland.

Beltaine bonfires were kindled solely with friction. Called a needfire, such a fire was considered sacred. In Ireland, a wheel and spindle were used to create the needfire; the wheel being an emblem of the sun and thus a perfect emblem for kindling a Beltaine blaze. On the islands of Skye, Mull, and Tiree off the coast of Scotland, a plank of oak featuring a hole bored through its center and an accompanying oak wimble were used. In some areas of Scotland, the friction was created with a square frame of green wood featuring an axle down the middle. Such contraptions were sometimes operated by multiple people working in teams. If any one of the party was guilty of murder, theft, adultery, or other heinous crimes, the fire would not start or its properties would be altogether void or significantly diminished. Once sparks were successfully created, a species of highly combustible agaric[1] that grows on birch trees was applied, causing an instant burst of flame from which the rest of the fire was kindled.

In Wales, even the gathering of the wood for the sacred Beltaine fire was performed with great ceremony. Nine men would be chosen to go into the woods to collect sticks and branches from nine different types of trees. Before they could do so, they had to empty their pockets of all money, coins, or other metal. After the wood had been gathered, a large circle was cut in the sod and the sacred sticks were placed in the middle and set ablaze.

The Beltaine fires were believed to have magickal properties. Their flames, their glowing embers, their ashes, and their smoke were all believed capable of granting health and protection. In the Isle of Man, the people invited the smoke of the bonfires to blow over themselves and their cattle, believing that this would ensure their mutual vitality. Once the fire died down, the ashes were sprinkled over the crops to increase the earth's fertility. Some theorists believe the fires were intended to mimic the sun and were thus used in an imitative sense to ensure an adequate supply of sunlight. Other theorists believe the fires were used instead in a sympathetic sense, the destructive property of the fire utilized to destroy any baneful influences—both natural and "supernatural"—that might otherwise threaten the health of people, animals, and crops.

One interesting custom practiced in the Scottish Highlands involved cooking a special oatmeal cake at the side of the great Beltaine fire. The cake was formed with nine raised knobs on its surface, and as the knobs were broken off one by one and tossed into the flames, they were offered up as sacrifice and appeasement to both livestock and threats to livestock alike.

One piece might be dedicated to the cattle, another piece to the fox, and so on, until the cake was all gone.

Another Scottish tradition involved an oatmeal cake being cooked in the fire and then divided into pieces equal to the number of people present. A piece of the cake was marked with charcoal and tossed into a bonnet along with the unmarred pieces. Blindfolded or with eyes closed, everyone would pick a piece of cake out of the bonnet. Whoever got the blackened piece became the unlucky victim of ridicule and a mock sacrifice. Termed the *cailleach beal-tine*, aka the "Beltaine *carline*" or the "Old Lady of Beltaine," the victim was either very briefly or very nearly tossed into the flames of the bonfire, or, alternatively, was forced to leap over the fire three times. He or she was afterward bombarded with a barrage of eggs and eggshells, and for the next several days, the victim was spoken about as if he or she were dead. This might sound unpleasant, but as history and archeology affords evidence of actual human sacrifice taking place in other Celtic lands like England, the *cailleach beal-tine* tradition seems relatively harmless.

Fire wasn't the only element believed to be especially potent at Beltaine. Water was also thought to have supernatural power. It was widely believed that the Beltaine morning dew was infused with magickal powers, capable of preserving youth, clearing skin ailments, and enhancing beauty and sexual attractiveness. Druids would collect the dew in a hollowed-out stone prior to sunrise on May Day morning. Whoever was sprinkled with this sacred dew could expect health and happiness. Young women would often roll in the dew on Beltaine morning or simply anoint their faces with the heavenly dew. Sometimes the dew was collected in a jar and left in the sunlight. It was then filtered and kept for use throughout the year as a versatile potion for beauty, healing, and more (MacLeod, 165).

Holy wells were also visited during the festival, and the first water drawn from a well on Beltaine morning was thought to be extremely potent and magickal. People would walk clockwise around the well to mimic the direction of the sun moving from east to west, then offerings of coins or other small tokens were given to the sacred well's residing spirit in hopes of gaining their favor and blessing. Sometimes small strips of clothing were thrown in the well with the aim of healing illness and other infirmities (Monaghan, 41–42).

Flowers also played a prominent role in Beltaine celebrations. Up until the late nineteenth century, it was common practice throughout Ireland, Scotland, and the Isle of Man to deck the halls and more with flowers come Beltaine. Yellow flowers were most often used, being the color symbolic of both fire and the sun. Primrose, hawthorn, rowan, marsh marigold, and gorse were frequently chosen for their colorful yellow blooms. Flowers were scattered on the threshold of the home as a means of ensuring magickal protection. Cows were also gussied up with flower garlands, and even the equipment used in the butter- and milk-making process received the same treatment.

Such customs were considered wise protection in light of the *sidhe,* a type of faerylike spirit believed to cause mischief. They were thought to be especially active on Beltaine (just as they are on Samhain), and dairy products often fell victim to their pranks. As an added precaution, small offerings of food and drink were placed at areas frequented by the *sidhe* in hopes of appeasing the spirits and avoiding their vengeance (MacLeod, 166). Other methods of fending off *sidhe* attacks included turning one's clothing inside out or carrying a small piece of iron, a substance long believed to have protective, witchcraft-negating qualities.

On the Isle of Man, the coming of May was celebrated for centuries with clockwise dancing in honor of the sun. Bushes were also burned across the island in hopes of banishing the witches and faeries believed to be taking refuge in the shrubbery.

As a festival, Beltaine had pretty much died out by the mid-twentieth century, but many of its customs were continued, blending in with more secular springtime celebrations. In recent years, the holiday has been revived in many places, celebrated as a community cultural event. Some traditions haven't needed reviving. In Arklow, Ireland, the Beltaine fire-making custom has continued into the present day, though it's not always taken as a sacred affair. In the May 5, 2005, edition of

*Wicklow People*, it was reported that some residents used the Beltaine fires as an opportunity to dispose of old furniture and other unwanted household goods, burning them in any of Arklow's several bonfires that raged throughout the May Eve night.

The Celts were but one of many cultures to honor the coming of May with ritual, ceremony, and magick. In fact, the earliest May Day-like celebrations we know of with certainty date all the way back to the time of ancient Rome. The Romans held an annual festival in honor of the goddess Flora at the end of April and beginning of May. In the Republican Era, the six-day festival started on April 27, and under the Julian calendar, it began on April 28. According to Ovid, the first ever Floralia, as the festival was called, was held in 238 BCE to commemorate the founding of the goddess Flora's temple, built on the advice of an oracle—the Sibylline Books—following a period of harsh drought (Futrell, 25–27). Flora was a goddess of fertility, vegetation, and flowers; a sacred lady in charge of the growing things. One of her monikers was the "Goddess of the Flowering of Plants." Imported from Greece, she was the Roman equivalent of Chloris, the Greek goddess of flowers.

Myths related to us by Ovid tell the story of Flora's divine birth. Flora, originally a nymph by the name of Chloris who resided in the heavenly land of Elysium, had gone out for a walk one fine spring day. Her indescribable beauty caught the attentions of Zephyrus, AKA the West Wind. Zephyrus wanted the beautiful nymph and began his pursuit. Chloris ran, but she could not outrun the wind. Chloris struggled, but she was no match for Zephyrus's strength. He raped her (some accounts tone it down to a kiss), and afterward made her his bride, granting her the title of Flora, goddess of all the flowering plants of the earth.

Other myths relate how Flora once helped the goddess Juno conceive a child by way of a magickal plant. As her myths reveal, Flora was closely associated with sexuality, fertility, and the blossoming of Nature. It was Flora, the myths tell us, who first spread seeds across the originally monochrome earth, causing it to bloom and blossom in an abundance of color and variety.

The Floralia festival held in Flora's honor included games, mimed performances, revelry, striptease, feasting, dancing, and an atmosphere of sexual liberty, pleasure, and wild abandon. At first, the Floralia was held only occasionally, at times when crops were deemed in danger. By 173 BCE, however, after a time of repeated and frequent crop issues, the Floralia became an annual event, believed to help ensure the favor of the goddess and encourage the fertility of the crops, livestock, and people.

Offerings of flower blossoms were made to Flora, and on the first of May, offerings were given in the name of Maia, a goddess of growth for whom the month of May is named. There was also a ceremony in which a number of hares and goats were released into the community arena to be hunted, the sexually active and ambitious animals believed to symbolize fertility. As another way to increase and encourage fertility, the festival crowd was showered with a barrage of "medals with obscene representations on them," vetches,[2] lupins,[3] and various beans all thought to symbolize fertile energies (Fowler, 94).

Flowers were an obvious and prominent feature of the Floralia, with blossoms decorating everything from the feasting tables to the citizenry. Garlands were hung on doors and wreaths of flowers were worn on the heads of the festivalgoers. Images of the goddess Flora were decked out in flower blossoms and carried in procession to the flowering trees.

Though ultimately a serious event expressing great reverence for Flora, the festival had a strong element of fun that predominated it. Lots of wine and lots of boisterous singing and dancing created an atmosphere of raucousness, the noise of which may have been believed to help Nature fully wake up and get energized after a long winter's slumber. It was customary to wear bright, multicolored clothing as opposed to the usual white. Promiscuity was also encouraged.

On the last day of the festival, a group of prostitutes would gather and perform a striptease in front of an audience. Other entertainments devised for the Floralia were equally exotic.

Galba, who served as Roman emperor from 68–69 CE, once hosted a tightrope-walking elephant at the celebration!

As the Roman Empire spread its cultural traditions throughout Europe, many Floralia customs were blended into pre-existing local springtime festivals. Many pre-Christian cultures considered May as the start of the summer season and marked the time with fertility rites and other ceremonious festivity. Over time, what was once sacred ritual became secular celebration, evolving into the local May Day customs that continue to be practiced throughout Europe and America. May Day became a composite of Roman and local tradition, just as our modern celebrations reflect a blending of traditions.

As a celebration of fertility and growth, May Day customs often centered around flowers, greenery, and sexual themes. It was common for young men and women to go into the woods on May Eve, emerging with arms full of foliage in the morning. Flowers and leafy branches were brought back to the village as a token of good will and to bring good luck. Sometimes, the villagers would throw flowers at one another. Boys often fashioned May-gads, wands crafted by stripping the bark off a stick of white willow and affixing some cowslips[4] to the top (Fosbroke, 651).

One once-popular European May Day custom that shows its ancient roots is the May doll. Children would make simple dolls out of natural items, or choose an existing doll, and dress it up with fresh flower blossoms. The May dolls were then paraded through town, just as the Romans carried their decorated image of Floralia through the streets of their Empire so long ago. Sometimes, the May doll was placed amidst a garland of greenery or secured into a structure comprised of two crossed hoops.

Another enduring May Day tradition that gained popularity in many parts of Europe was the May Bush. Usually a small thorn tree, the May Bush was decorated with flowers, ribbons, and brightly painted shells or bits of colorful fabric. There were household May Bushes that were placed outside the home, and there were communal May Bushes located in public common areas. Sometimes the May Bush was paraded around the neighborhood for all to see. Dancing around the May Bush was thought to be an effective means of ensuring good fortune, perhaps a throwback to ancient tree worship reflecting a belief in the magickal power of the residing tree spirit.

In some places, such as Dublin and Belfast, it became tradition for the entire community to decorate their May Bushes together, with neighborhood districts enjoying the friendly competition of attempting to create the best-looking May Bush. The competitive spirit often progressed into mischief, with neighborhood groups often stealing the May Bush of their rivals. The practice became such a problem in some places that in Victorian times, the May Bush was actually outlawed.

Very similar to the May Bush is the Maypole. Generally formed from a tall tree that's been stripped of its branches, the Maypole has obvious phallic symbolism. Originally decorated with flowers and greenery, the traditional Maypole was a representation of fertile energies and a focal point for springtime celebration. As with the May Bush, the Maypole was often placed at the center of town, and townsfolk often tried to steal the Maypoles of neighboring communities. There was a spirit of friendly competition as everyone vied for the unofficial honor of having the biggest, best Maypoles in the region.

After the Maypole was erected and decorated, dances were held around it in the belief of inviting growth, fertility, and other springtime blessings. In the Victorian period, ribbons came to be an essential part of the Maypole decorations, and Maypole dancing became more elaborate as a result. Dancers would hold the ends of the ribbons and weave around each other in intricate figures, braiding the ribbon around the pole as the dance proceeded.

Maypole dances were once common throughout Europe and eventually migrated to America, with many such celebrations continuing into modern times despite periodic objections. The Puritans once denounced the Maypole as a "heathenish vanity of superstition and wickedness," and when Thomas Morton erected an eighty-foot-tall Maypole complete with a set of antlers attached to the top on the shores of Boston in 1627, he was soon arrested by the local authorities and denounced as the "Lord of Misrule." The Maypole custom understandably died down for a time in America after that, but around the time of the Revolutionary War, Maypoles were once again erected as "Liberty Poles" and became the focal point for May Day eve war dances and celebration.

Eventually, Maypoles became common May Day fare in America. At a celebration held in 1833 in Boston, a fifteen-foot-tall Maypole was erected and decorated with evergreens, roses, and garlands. Around the same time, Maypole dancing became popular at women's colleges, adopted as a means of physical education and a way to support overall good health and fertility. In the early 1900s, Maypole dancing as physical education was introduced to the New York City school system and was soon implemented in other large urban school districts. As a result, the celebration of May Day made great gains in popularity among children. At New York's fiftieth annual May Day celebration held in 1957, more than 12,000 children took part in the ceremonies that featured multiple Maypoles, all painted a sparkling gold (Lyons, 139–144).

One widespread European May Day tradition that never became very established in America was the crowning of the May Queen, who with her floral crown, clearly bears close resemblance to the goddess Flora, who wore an identical mark of station. The May Queen traditionally wears a white gown, a symbol of purity, and a crown formed of fresh flower blossoms. As the personification of the festival and all it symbolizes, the May Queen is in charge of representing fertility, beauty, and youthfulness. She may be called on to make speeches, lead parades, or perform other related duties according to local custom. Many localities would choose their own May Queen to preside over the May Day festivities, selecting a young maiden on whom to bestow the honor. Sometimes the children present chose the May Queen, and she was generally selected for her beauty, pleasantness, and innocence.

Sometimes, a May King was chosen as well, with some traditions pairing the May Queen with the May King as her consort. This custom may have its roots in more ancient Pagan practice, symbolic of the mythological annual union between goddess and god, and symbolic of the earth's fertilization and subsequent blossoming due to interaction between the earth and the sun.

The May Queen and May King weren't the only ones for whom amorous opportunities existed. One custom involved young people going into the forest together on the eve of May Day for the primary purpose of engaging in amorous entertainments. Lovers would hook up in the woods and spend the night together, returning home in the morning with armfuls of fresh greenery with which to decorate the village. In some places, the resulting partnerships were termed Greenwood marriages. Traditionally, the start of May is a popular time for handfasting, and sometimes Greenwood marriages and other pairings were made permanent in an official wedding ceremony. Handfasting might involve binding the couple's hands together, jumping the broom, or jumping the cauldron.

Another widespread and prominent May Day tradition was the May Basket. On the first of May, children would leave small baskets of flowers, candies, or other goodies on the doorknobs of their friends and neighbors as a token of friendship and good-will. The custom of leaving May Baskets became quite popular in England, and as the English settled America, the practice came with them. Although prevailing Puritanical viewpoints confined May Day to a fairly secular event in America, the May Basket tradition persisted, only beginning to die out around the mid-twentieth century. A newspaper article from the April 24, 1952, edition of the *Prescott Evening Courier* relates:

"That old American custom of hanging a May basket on the door of a friend on May Day seems to be dying out. Yet, in the lifetime of most people, it has been more popular than the custom of sending Christmas cards."

Another European May Day tradition that eventually found its way to America is Morris dancing. Popularly practiced in the late 1700s and mid-1800s in England, Morris dancing was a special figure dance that was often performed in conjunction with May Day celebrations. Dancers often wield props, such as hand-kerchiefs or sticks, while weaving intricate patterns and creating choreographed figures through their rhythmic steps and movements. Morris dancers traditionally wore costumes consisting of white pants, white shirts, hats decked out with ribbons and flowers, and brass bells attached to their legs, but sometimes other costumes were worn by the dancers chosen to take on special roles in the performance. As a ritual folk dance, Morris dancing often included heavily theatrical elements. One of the dancers might don an animal disguise, and at a certain point in the performance they would act like they were dying. The other dancers would crowd around in attendance, and when the animal-man was inevitably resurrected, they would dance joyfully in celebration. Such performances seem to mimic Nature's revival and were thought to bring good luck to the community.

Such magickal and theatrical elements reflect Morris dancing's association with the mummers play, another sort of ritualistic performance that was also incorporated into European seasonal celebrations. The basic framework for the mummers play generally featured a hero or a champion who was slain in a fight then brought back to life by an attending doctor. Mummers plays are believed to have their roots in the custom of "momerie" that dates back as early as the thirteenth century. Groups of masked revelers, called "mummers," would travel in silence from house to house, entering the home to dance or play a game of dice, all the while remaining completely speechless. Over time, as "momerie" blended into and merged with other cultural practices, the full-fledged mummers play developed.

With its basic theme of death and resurrection, the mummers play became a fitting accompaniment for agriculturally themed celebrations such as May Day.

Many European May Day celebrations still include heavily theatrical elements such as the mummers play or the Morris dance, complete with a full cast of characters acting out significant aspects of springtime myth. English villages such as Somerset and Padstow celebrate May Day with a mummers play featuring a hobbyhorse or a pair of hobbyhorses in the starring role. The hobbyhorses are usually men dressed in masks and holding stick ponies between their legs. Skirting is added to conceal the stick, so that it appears like the hobbyhorse is a full-bodied animal. In places where two hobbyhorses are used, the horses often take on the roles of summer and winter. The summer hobbyhorse and the winter hobbyhorse act out mock battles, with the summer horse always eventually prevailing.

In Padstow, there was originally only one hobbyhorse, called the "old 'oss" or "old horse." In the 1840s, bystanders would sometimes be smeared with lamp black or soot by the "old 'oss" as part of the festivities, and it was believed to bring good luck to touch the hobbyhorse's tar-stained, sailcloth skirts. As part of the play act, the "old 'oss" would feign death, only to get back up, resurrected and reenergized in an apparent imitation of springtime renewal. A second horse was added to the

Padstow celebration at the time of World War I. Donning patriotic colors and decked out with springtime blossoms, this horse is called the "peace 'oss," or "peace horse." The "peace horse," taking on the role of summer, canters around the festivalgoers searching for a mate. An atmosphere of fun prevails as the horse "captures" women, bringing them under the skirts of the horse costume. If so captured, it was once believed, the woman could expect to become pregnant within the year.

The hobbyhorses aren't the only characters in the May Day cast. Many mummers plays or Morris dancing theatrics also featured a Fool or a Teaser and a handful of other personalities whose connections to springtime rites are seldom remembered. Robin Hood and Maid Marian, for instance, whose best-known myths center on forbidden love and robbing the rich to give to the poor, were central figures at English May Day celebrations in the medieval and Tudor periods. Clad in green, Robin Hood became a symbol of the light, warmth, and luscious foliage of summer, the hero come to bring redemption out of the depths of winter's darkness and lack. Maid Marian, who accompanied Robin Hood as a central character at many May Day celebrations, took on the role of a sort of May Queen or Lady of the May, a beautiful maiden come to usher in the warmer season. As traditional Morris dancing didn't allow for female dancers, Maid Marian was often played by a man in cross-dress. Maid Marian may have her origins in a French tale about a shepherdess and her lover, who incidentally happened to be a shepherd named Robin.

There's also the Jack in the Green, a living, breathing personification of a forest god or nature spirit come to deliver humankind from the cold season. In the sixteenth and seventeenth centuries, May Day celebrations in England often included a Jack in the Green who would don a conical framework that was covered completely in foliage, concealing most of his body in a mass of vegetation. The Jack in the Green character was expected to be loud, drunk, and raucous, and as such, the character fell out of favor in the more prudish and proper Victorian period.

Although the European population was largely Christianized by the time the mummers play and the Morris dance became established, these folk traditions continued to reflect much older Pagan elements, alluding to themes of Nature's annual cycles of death, resurrection, and fertility.

Another May celebration worthy of note is Walpurgis Night, a Germanic festival held April 30 or May 1 throughout much of Central and Northern Europe. The earliest mention of Walpurgis Night is found in a 1603 edition of a text called the *Calendarium Perpetuum* by Johann Coler, but the holiday likely has earlier origins. Essentially a spring celebration marking the end of winter, Walpurgis Night is named after a female English missionary who was canonized on May 1, 870 CE, as Saint Walpurga. Because of the date of her canonization, Saint Walpurga became associated with May rites and traditions, and the eve before May Day came to be known as Walpurgis Night, or *Walpurgisnacht* in the German and Dutch. Walpurgis Night was celebrated with bonfires, dancing, and rituals intended to ward off malicious witchcraft and other perceived threats. It was a time when witches were believed to gather on hilltops to light fires and usher in the arrival of spring. In some places, Walpurgis Night was celebrated as the "burning of the witches." Faux "witches" made from cloth and straw, or sometimes broomsticks, were thrown into the bonfires and burned. This custom was intended to bring a symbolic end to the winter while at the same time effectively banishing evil or supernatural influences that might otherwise cause harm.

In Sweden, Walpurgis Night is celebrated as Valborg, and it's traditionally marked with dancing, singing, bonfires, and trick-or-treating. One very old Swedish custom rarely practiced in modern times was for young people to go to the woods at twilight to gather greenery and branches that were later brought back to the village and placed on homes as decoration. The party would sing songs, and the householders were expected to pay for the unsolicited service with eggs.

Throughout the ages, early May rituals and traditions have blended, creating a garden of possibility and a rich tapestry of eclectic customs. Beltane is a celebration of fertility and growth and of the sun's increasing warmth and light. The ancients found a plethora of ways to honor the holiday through rituals, magick, and many other means. We modern Pagans can enjoy even greater diversity as our Beltane represents a conglomeration of the May-tide wisdom that's accumulated over thousands of years. Celebrating the coming of May is tradition, even when we make those traditions our own.

NEW WAYS

tection, purification, manifestation, handfastings, building sacre

visiting sacred wells, giving offerings, working with faeries, vita

alking the boundaries of one's property, protecting plants, divin

animals, people, and possessions astronomical midpoint, and sun

n the spring equinox and summer solstice: Sun at 15 degrees of

in the northern hemisphere, Sun at 15 degrees of Scorpio in

outhern hemisphere. Female: Maiden Goddess, Mother Godd

Earth Goddess, water plants or animals, the Lover preparin

with her beloved Flora, Danu, Freyya, Maia, Shasti, Pro-

Chin-hua fu-jen, Venus, Diana, Artemis, Aphrodite, Astar

Bona, Rauni, Sarasvati, Horae, Pan, Cernunnos, Beal, Bat,

Pluto, Wotan, Odin, Oak King, Apollo, Ra, Mugwort, L

fertility, protection, divination, communication, with spirits ene

purification, joy, love, prophetic dreams, renewal energy, vitalit

wealth, fairy magick, luck success, strength Rose, Frankincen

Jasmine, Lemon, Pine, Mint visiting sacred wells, giving off

faeries, abundance, growth, passion, love, union, cooperation, fert

tection, purification, manifestation, handfastings, building sacre

$\mathcal{W}$HILE MODERN PAGAN practice is often very different from that of our ancient Pagan ancestors, our Beltane celebrations are nonetheless reflective of timeless beliefs and traditions that have endured throughout the ages. As Nature abounds in all her springtime glory, it's only natural to rejoice and celebrate the warm sunshine, the beautiful flowers, and the growing plants that will soon ripen to feed and nourish the masses. Beltane is a time to celebrate the spring and summer, a time to honor the increasing strength of the sun and the longer days and warmth that it brings. As Nature blossoms, so too does the human spirit, and we may become more energized and frisky as Beltane approaches. Love is often on our minds, and lusty thoughts frequently occupy our moments as we find ourselves in a mood for fun, excitement, magick, and more.

## Modern Themes and Common Elements

While Beltane celebrations and customs vary from place to place and from individual to individual, there are many common themes and similar elements. Festivities tend to have a lighthearted and raucous feel, and rituals generally focus on fertility, prosperity, health, protection, purification, and growth as the summer season is ushered in. Spellwork tends to gravitate toward themes of love, passion, and romance, and sex magick is a favorite technique. Music, dancing, feasting, singing, picnicking, and fireside rituals and get-togethers are frequently incorporated into Beltane celebrations, and flowers and vegetation are used universally as a symbol of Nature's abundance and fertility. Most Beltane celebrations are held outdoors where possible, with merrymaking and magick taking place throughout the night and day. Sex, love, laughter, romance, and celebration of the spring and summer season take center stage, and nature walks, picnics, potlucks, Maypole dances, and romantic games are popular activities.

## Beltane in the Country

Pagans in rural areas might celebrate Beltane with rituals focused on celebrating Nature's fertility and ensuring the well-being and protection of one's family, homestead, and property. Large fires are often lit, and magickal rituals intended to protect livestock and crops may be performed. Some people drive their livestock between two fires in an attempt to protect the animals from disease and injury, just like the ancient Celts did. It's also a common practice to walk around the boundaries of one's property, performing protective rituals and uttering blessings as the circuit is made. Homes and altars are often decorated with wildflowers and other vegetation native to the local area, freshly harvested in the wild by the rural practitioner just in time for Beltane. Most rural Pagans celebrate Beltane alone or with small groups comprised of immediate family and perhaps a few nearby friends and neighbors.

## Beltane in the City

Urban Pagans who have the advantages of city living have some obstacles to face when it comes to celebrating Beltane. For starters, it can be difficult to find a place to build a Beltane bonfire when you're surrounded by skyscrapers and traffic jams. For another, vegetation in the city is often sparse, and communing with Nature in the concrete jungle can be a bit of a struggle. These challenges are no match for the resourceful modern Pagan, however, and city witches have found creative ways around these difficulties. Candles and fireplaces are used in place of bonfires, for instance, while a quick trip to the florist can yield a bounty of real-life foliage to deck both the halls and the ritual space. Sometimes, artificial flowers are used in lieu of fresh vegetation. For many city Pagans, Beltane celebrations are held indoors or in a community park. Since most urban dwellers don't grow crops or raise livestock, Beltane rituals are typically focused on more personal goals, such as self-improvement, creative fertility, purification, and romance. Houseplants and pets may feature into magick and ritual, giving a natural touch to urban workings. More and more urban areas today have open and established Pagan communities, and Beltane rituals and get-togethers are common in many of America's larger cities.

## Different Pagans, Different Practices

Here is a sampling of several Pagan "denominations," and a brief look at some ways those particular denominations might choose to celebrate Beltane. Keep in mind however that Pagans are a diverse bunch, and even amongst the practitioners of the same Pagan paths and traditions, there is still great difference in practice and belief from group to group and from individual to individual.

### Celtic Reconstructionist

Celtic Reconstructionists aim to practice early Celtic religion as accurate to history as possible. They often time their Beltane celebrations by observing visible signs in Nature. When the local hawthorn trees begin to flower, it can be interpreted as a signal that Beltane time has arrived. Alternatively, Beltane may be celebrated on the first full moon following the blossoming of the hawthorns, or timed to coincide with the date when the sun is at fifteen degrees Taurus. Many Celtic Reconstructionists refer to Beltane by its Gaelic name, *Lá Bealtaine*.

Like the Celts themselves, Celtic Reconstructionists typically mark Beltane with ritual bonfires. Two bonfires are lit and livestock, pets, and people are passed between them to ensure blessings and protection. Afterward, candles might be lit from the main fire and brought home, a reflection of the original Celtic tradition of relighting the hearth fires from the sacred Beltane flames. In urban areas where bonfires aren't possible, modern practitioners may substitute with torches or candles.

Feasting and general merrymaking are also popular traditions, and traditional Celtic foods and beverages are sometimes prepared. Flowering tree branches might be brought inside the home, and rowan crosses are often hung on the wall as a means of gaining magickal protection. Once widely known and commonly praised throughout the British Isles as a protective charm, a rowan cross is an equal-armed cross made from two pieces of rowan wood, which is often tied in the middle with a piece of red thread. May bushes may also be used, and deities are honored. Celtic Reconstructionists might also celebrate Beltane by visiting wells, where prayers or praises to the spirit of the well may be uttered and offerings are left behind.

## Wiccan

Wicca is a Witchcraft tradition introduced near the middle of the twentieth century and based on Pre-Christian religion, animistic belief, and shamanic principles and practices. Most Wiccans revere a male deity known as the Horned God, and a female, triple-aspected deity known as the Triple Goddess. Her three aspects are referred to as the Maiden, the Mother, and the Crone. Most Wiccans tend to be eclectic in their practices, and while certain traditional methods or guidelines might be adhered to, there is usually plenty of room for personalization, improvisation, and creativity. Wiccan Beltane celebrations typically focus on fertility and sexuality, though themes of abundance, protection, purification, or growth might also be prevalent. Maypole dances often take center stage, and many local groups host large community get-togethers. There's usually a bonfire or two, along with a fair amount of revelry, merrymaking, and mayhem.

Though the holiday is approached with great reverence, an atmosphere of fun and frivolity prevails. Bawdy behavior becomes appropriate, friendly flirtation is smiled on, and openly sexual discourse becomes standard. In some covens, the high priestess and high priest reenact the Beltane myth of the young lusty god mating with the fertile maiden goddess, bringing new life and renewal to the earth. Sometimes this reenactment involves ritual sex, but many groups today stick with a more symbolic representation of the myth, performing actions meant only to imitate the sex act. For example, a wand or scepter might be plunged into a cup in imitation of sexual penetration, the cup representing the female energy and the wand or scepter representing the male energy. Whether literal or symbolic, this ritual union serves a holy purpose: to bring the practitioners a deeper experiential understanding of the earth's fertilization and blossoming after the darker part of the year has passed.

Though skyclad is sometimes the preferred fashion, ritual clothing is often worn at Wiccan Beltane celebrations, with flower garlands and brightly colored clothing the norm. Green and yellow predominate, but pink, white, and other pastel colors invoking spring, purity, and romance are also used. The home and the altar are often given the same treatment, dressed in flowers and the colors of spring.

Solitary Wiccans may do a meditation, enjoying some time in solitude in the sunshine or using a candle as a focal point for nighttime practice. Prayers may be said, and offerings may be given to the God and the Goddess, and sometimes to the faeries. These offerings typically come in the form of food, water, flowers, and herbs.

Rituals are often more elaborate and formal in comparison to more frequently practiced esbat proceedings, and the tone is usually joyful, reverent, and celebratory. Honor is given to the Goddess and God, as evocations and/or invocations are spoken.

Magick is often incorporated into the Beltane ritual, with love, romance, abundance, growth, and prosperity common themes for spells, charms, and magickal crafts. It's a popular time for divination, and Wiccans may use any variety of tools and systems such as tarot, runes, pendulums, or the I Ching to discern the general outlook for health, wealth, love, and overall success.

## Heathen

Heathenry encompasses Asatru and other Neopagan paths that practice the pre-Christian religious traditions of Germany, Scandinavia, and other places in northern Europe. While May Day celebrations aren't among the most important holidays of the Heathen year, many modern Heathens do mark the occasion, celebrating the Germanic holiday of Walburg, or Walpurgis Night, on April 30, and celebrating May Day on May 1. It's a time when magick is believed to be afoot, a time when spirits wander. Heathens today may mark the occasion with a great bonfire, a simple feast, and liberal toasts made to the god Wotan (aka Odin) and to the goddesses of magick.

## (Modern) Druid

Unlike Celtic Reconstructionists who strive to follow the historical religion of the ancient Celts as closely as is feasible, modern Druids are more of the Celtic Revivalist style, picking and choosing from ancient Celtic beliefs and adapting these for current times. Contemporary Druids are often eclectic, merging various traditions and new inventions with the time-honored practices of the ancient Celts. Modern Druids may mark Beltane with a ritual in honor of the goddess Danu, the earth mother, and the god Belenos, the sun king. Beltane is seen as a time to celebrate fertility, union, and sexuality. It's a time of protection and purification, and it's a time to honor the dead. Faeries are believed to make extra mischief on Beltane, the veil between the worlds thinning at this time just as it does on Samhain. Some modern Druids may wear bells to help keep the naughty faeries at bay. Prayers for health, prosperity, protection, and love may be made, and offerings of bread, beer, or mead are left for the gods and the dead.

## *Traditional Witchcraft*

Traditional Witchcraft is the religion of non-Wiccan witches who base their practices on pre-Christian animism, traditional folk magick, and an often polytheistic belief system. Traditional Witchcraft varies from place to place, and specific practices are based on the local culture and the environment in which one lives. Some Traditional witches celebrate the solstices and equinoxes, and some celebrate the four cross-quarter days, but most do not celebrate both. Traditionally, either the solstices and equinoxes were honored, or the cross-quarter days were honored, according to local lifestyles and to the needs of the land. Traditions that were mostly agricultural tend to celebrate the solstices and equinoxes, while more pastoral-based traditions with their roots in Celtic lands acknowledge the cross-quarter days such as Beltane. When Traditional witches celebrate Beltane, they may do so just as their ancestors did, with bonfires, rituals, orgiastic revelry, reverence, and magick.

## *Neopagan*

Neopaganism is a term defining a broad and varied category of practitioners engaged in any number of forms of nature-based spirituality or new takes on old Pagan religions and practices. Neopagans include Wiccans, eclectic witches, modern Druids, and others—nearly anyone living in modern times who defines themselves as a Pagan is also a Neopagan by definition, as it essentially means "new Pagan."

Neopagans may celebrate Beltane alone or with a group. Many communities today have open Neopagan social groups that bring together people from a variety of paths. Daytime Beltane picnics are popular, and groups often gather at public parks, mountainsides, riversides, and other pleasant outdoor locations. Potlucks are the standard, with everyone bringing a dish to share. Often, groups enjoy a nature walk together either before or after the feast. Depending on the group, rituals and magick might also be performed, which range in both formality and form.

Solitary Neopagans might choose to celebrate Beltane in a traditional way, recreating the practices of a particular path or system, or they may decide to get creative, crafting their own

Beltane proceedings based on personal taste, need, ability, and intuition, completely independent of any established method.

## *Eclectic Witchcraft*

Eclectic Witchcraft is a term defining practitioners of Witchcraft who may or may not choose to define themselves as Wiccan, and who draw practices and beliefs from a variety of traditions and from both personally crafted and indigenous magickal and spiritual systems. Common aspects include an emphasis on natural energies and seasonal tides, with most eclectic witches working closely with the moon, the sun, the stars, the earth, and the elements.

Beltane rituals often emphasize springtime energies, and fires may be lit in solidarity with the sun's rising strength. Common themes include abundance, growth, prosperity, fertility, love, and sexuality. Rituals are typically very joyful, and fresh vegetation such as leaves and flowers are frequently found donning the altar as well as the witches. Sometimes plants are all that is worn on the body, and, of course, there are many eclectic witches who prefer to wear nothing at all.

Many eclectic witches consider Beltane the perfect time to honor the union of energies that manifests the blossoming of Nature, and sex magick may be practiced solo, with a partner, or with multiple partners. Sex magick can have a strongly magickal focus or a highly reverent tone with the ritual serving the sole purpose of communion with the divine, no particular magickal goal at hand. It might take the form of one person receiving stimulation from the group, directing the energy raised toward a shared magickal goal. It might take the form of one partner representing the lunar Triple Goddess and one partner representing the solar Horned God who impregnates her. (This impregnation is understood in a magickal and metaphorical sense; birth control and safe sex are wisely practiced.) Sex magick can take the form of a solitary witch self-stimulating while invoking the god of the spring. Practices vary, as eclectic witches are by definition diverse.

## *Modern Beltane Gatherings and Festivals*

Here's a sampling of some modern Beltane festivals worth visiting. Although most are ultimately secular celebrations, all have strong elements of magick and/or ritual, making them quite suitable events for a Pagan wanting to enjoy a good time for Beltane.

### *Beltane Fire Festival—Edinburgh, Scotland*

Held on Calton Hill on the night of April 30, the Beltane Fire Festival is a modern arts and cultural event organized by the Beltane Fire Society, a community arts performance charity. The festival is described as "investigative theatre," with both planned and spontaneous theatrical performances, drumming, and ritual taking place throughout the night at various places on the hill. A great procession led by the May Queen circles the hill, and a symbolic reenactment of the death and rebirth of the Green Man is held. Participants are urged to follow the sound of the drumming to find spontaneous revelers and impromptu performances throughout the park. The celebration attracts a crowd of more than twelve thousand people each year.

### Beltania—Florence, Colorado

Beltania is a Pagan celebration and music festival held in early May in the mountains of Colorado. The four-day festival features camping, rituals, workshops, live music, and a very large-scale Maypole dance featuring more than one hundred ribbons. A Green Man and a May Queen are crowned and celebrated. Drum circles and dancing keep everyone busy well into the night, and a skyclad camping area open only to attendees who are eighteen years of age or older provides endless opportunity for magick and mischief in the dark. Bardic circles, spontaneous singing, and storytelling around the campfire add to the atmosphere of fun and fellowship that prevails throughout the festival. Beltania is hosted by Living Earth, an open Neopagan group and community church offering rituals, family events, classes, and other services in the Denver metro area.

## *May Day Parade and Festival—Minneapolis, Minnesota*

For more than forty years, the Twin Cities have come together for a community-wide celebration of May Day that includes a parade, a ceremony, and a festival. Parade participants and spectators number over fifty thousand each year, coming from both near and far. Puppets, dancers, and performers donning giant masks—some over ten feet tall—fill the streets, and music, joy, and laughter fill the air. The parade also features a Free Speech section, where community groups march in proclamation of their respective causes.

May Day festivities in Minneapolis also include a large public ceremony to help awaken the slumbering summer. A pageant featuring dancers, live orchestra music, and four giant puppets representing the prairie, sky, river, and woods is enjoyed by the all-ages audience. More than two hundred participants take part in the pageant. The pageant culminates in drumming, while a red sun flotilla, a type of flat-bottomed boat, is paddled across a lake to awaken the Tree of Life that sleeps on the opposite shore. This is called the Tree of Life ceremony, and people of all ages participate.

The festival that follows the May Day Parade and Tree of Life Ceremony features live bands, dancing, food, poetry readings, informational booths hosted by local grassroots organizations, canoe rides, and more.

## *May Day Fairie Festival—Spoutwood Farm Outside of Glen Rock, Pennsylvania*

The May Day Fairie Festival is an annual event held in early May at an organic farm located just outside of Glen Rock, Pennsylvania. The event celebrates the arrival of summer weather and the return of the faeries and other nature spirits to the world of warmth and sunshine now that the freeze of winter has officially thawed. With arts and crafts, live music, dancing, storytelling, faery and gnome habitat tours, faery tea parties, a Maypole, and more, the three-day family-friendly festival attracts more than sixteen thousand people each year.

## *Blue Ridge Beltane Festival—Greenville, Virginia*

The Blue Ridge Beltane Festival features rituals, drumming, workshops, vendors, bands, fire spinners, and more for a three-day camping event in honor of the coming of summer. Highlights include the lighting of the Bel-Fire, the Maypole dance, and the Inner Sanctum—an area of the camp devoted to workshops, rituals, and impromptu encounters emphasizing the sacred sexual experience. The Inner Sanctum is only open to consensual adults ages eighteen and older who wish to explore the more sacred and magickal side of human sexuality. There is also a youth zone featuring kid-friendly arts, crafts, imaginative games, rituals, and other activities appropriate for the younger set.

## The Beltane Gathering—Darlington, Maryland

The Beltane Gathering is a five-day celebration of sacred sexuality and personal freedom held on a 200-acre retreat center in Darlington, Maryland, during the first week of May. Group rituals, workshops, and presentations on sacred sex topics and a sensual feast are highlights of this camping event and magickal retreat. Vendors selling sex toys and magickal tools peddle their wares.

Attendees sleep in cabins or tents, but with all the opportunities for fun the festival affords, resting often takes a low priority. As the festival centers around celebrating sexual liberation and utilizing the tremendous power and potential that lies therein, public sex is allowed, and kink is welcome.

## Beltain Festival—Butser Ancient Farm
## near Petersfield, Hampshire, England

Each year, the Butser Ancient Farm near Petersfield in the English countryside hosts a Beltane ritual and celebration that draws a crowd of all ages. The festivities include a hog roast, picnicking, and live music. Children craft flower and wicker crowns to don, and they parade them about proudly as families picnic on the lawn. When nighttime falls, all eyes shift to the star of the show—a thirty-foot-tall wicker man soon to be set ablaze. Festivalgoers write down their hopes and wishes on small scraps of paper, which are stuffed inside the human-shaped wicker framework. The wicker man is lit, and the crowd watches eagerly as the flames rise higher, soon engulfing the whole contraption and eventually causing it to collapse to the ground in a heap of burnt twigs and ashes. The burning of the wicker man symbolizes the end of winter and a promise that summer is on the way. As could be expected, the ritual is met with great rejoicing, loud noise, and raucous celebration.

## Beltane—Thornborough Henge near Ripon, North Yorkshire, England

Thornborough Henge, a prehistoric site in north Yorkshire, has been the site of an annual Beltane celebration since 2004. Featuring a May Day fool, a mystery play, and a fire-lighting ceremony, the free gathering aims to offer an alternative to more commercial Beltane festivals. With Brigantia, a goddess once revered in the old kingdom of northern England, as a focal point of the ceremonies, Beltane at Thornborough Henge has a distinctly unique, local flavor. Revelers often camp out the night before the main events, enjoying the magickal, mystical atmosphere that the historic site provides. The largest group of prehistoric earthworks in Britain, the Thornborough Henges is comprised of an extensive landscape of henges, stone monuments, and Cursus (parallel sets of banks flanked by ditches) formed to run alongside or over top ancient barrows. The site is dated to the Neolithic period, its construction likely beginning and ending sometime between 3000 and 2000 BCE.

Many couples choose Beltane at Thornborough Henge as the ideal occasion to get married, and handfasting by means of jumping over a fire, jumping over a broom, or literally binding together the hands of the lovers can be witnessed by all in attendance. Costumes are encouraged at the celebration, with flower garlands as a popular choice for Beltane garb. Drumming, fire rituals, fun, fellowship, and the ever-present chance for Beltane romance draw a crowd of more than five hundred attendees from throughout the region.

## Modern Secular Celebrations

Today, many communities honor May Day with secular celebrations the whole town can enjoy. Though the atmosphere and tone are more focused on entertainment than on spirituality or magick, definite remnants of ancient Pagan practice can certainly be discerned in the proceedings.

Many towns in the UK host community May Day festivals, often centered around a grand Maypole. Bonfire rituals are still traditional, and in Limerick, Ireland, community bonfire ceremonies have continuously been practiced Beltane after Beltane all the way into modern times.

Walpurgis night is celebrated in places throughout Central and Northern Europe, with spring festivals held on April 30 or May 1. Fireside dancing, feasting, and merrymaking are prevalent aspects of the festivities.

In Germany, Walpurgis Night and May Day are celebrated on April 30 and May 1. On Walpurgis Night, bonfires are lit and fireside rituals focused on purification may be performed. Celebrations of spring's arrival tend to get rowdy, and pranks are common. These pranks are often virtually harmless acts such as rearranging things or swapping one neighbor's patio set for another neighbor's outdoor furniture, but more raucous and malicious pranks are not uncommon.

May Day is also considered a time to honor and stand up for worker's rights, and rallies, marches, and other demonstrations are held in many localities. Many communities have a Maypole that is given a place of prominence. Public festivals are held to celebrate the spring.

Smaller "maypoles" are also used. This tradition gives a branch decorated in colorful ribbons as a token of love. Traditionally, the branch was to be placed in the garden of the desired lover as a declaration of affection, the action believed to bring good luck in gaining the person's romantic interest. Many people spend time outdoors on May Day, enjoying the sunshine and looking forward to warmer days to come.

In the Czech Republic, April 30 is a time for purification and celebration. Straw and cloth are fashioned into the form of a "witch," which is then tossed into a fire in a symbolic burning of all things dark and dismal. Sometimes brooms are used in place of the "witches." Large meals are often enjoyed near a bonfire, and dancing and singing generally ensue. May 1 is celebrated as a day of love, and couples often visit local parks together.

In Estonia, Spring Day celebrations begin at sundown on the night of April 30 and continue through the day of May 1. The atmosphere is like a carnival, and streets are filled with revelers dressed as witches in reflection of a long-standing superstition suggesting the night is a time when real witches gather en masse for ritual and magick-making. It's a time to celebrate the arrival of spring, and both magick and mayhem are in the air. The humbler classes enjoy a little extra regard on Spring Day, with students and many workers honored with a day off.

In Finland, May is ushered in with large parties and public celebrations. Parades are held for the wider community to enjoy, and smaller groups of friends, families, and students gather for picnics. A mead-like beverage called sima is often served.

May Day is also celebrated in Newfoundland, where it is still local custom in some places to decorate a May Bush, decking out a small tree or shrub with brightly colored ribbons and other trimmings meant to herald in and celebrate the spring.

On the first day of May in France, Lily of the Valley is sold all along the streets, the flower being a symbol of springtime believed to attract good luck. One legend holds that the flower first sprang into existence when Eve was exiled from the Garden of Eden. It's said that wherever Eve's tears fell, a Lily of the Valley burst up from the earth. May Day is also the national Labour Day, called the *Fête du Travail*. Demonstrations for worker's rights are held, and working classes celebrate a day off as banks and most stores close shop for this national holiday.

## Suggested Activities

Beltane is a time of fertility, creativity, and growth. It's a time to renew our connection to the natural world, and a time to celebrate our role in manifesting that world. As we witness the fruits of Nature grow and thrive right before our eyes, Beltane reminds us that we are every bit as dependent on the earth's fertility as were our ancestors.

As the tenders of the crops, as the caretakers of the animals, as the conscious beings who set the boundaries of possibility, we humans have an important job to do in ensuring our own survival. Not only must we care for the earth and ourselves with our physical bodies and mundane actions, but also we must use our magickal abilities to expand the limits of perception and potential in order to allow greater beauty and a bigger bounty to manifest.

While we understand full well that the sun doesn't depend on sacrifices being made or fires being lit in order to shine, when we operate as if Nature depends on us, it makes us feel a little better and more secure, more in control than does the more obvious reality of us humans being utterly dependent on Nature. We are dependent on Nature, without a doubt, but at the same time, we are ourselves a part of Nature, and we therefore have the ability to influence it. We simply feel more connected and empowered when we supplement our physical, mundane actions with a little magick, and Beltane is a great opportunity to do so. Here are a few suggested Beltane activities that will help you magickally tune in to the season through both mundane and mystical action.

## Review Your Defenses

The ancient Celts of long ago may have felt a wee bit safer after performing their Beltane fire rites intended to purify and protect their animals, just as we modern Pagans today find comfort in doing whatever we can magickally to help ensure and safeguard our success. Whether it's an extra charm placed over a perfectly sufficient deadbolt lock or a crystal placed in the soil of an already healthy and thriving plant, we like to do all we can to gain magickal protection, and with its strong solar energies, Beltane offers a perfect opportunity for protective magickal workings.

Consider reviewing your defenses this Beltane, both the magickal and the mundane. You might inspect your home's window and door locks, making repairs where needed. Then, hang a small piece of hawthorn over each entrance as an added magickal protection. You might also take an honest look at your personal habits and lifestyle, and if you often find yourself in dangerous situations or engaging in risky behavior, consider adopting extra precautions. For instance, do you walk alone at night when you could instead walk with a buddy? Would it be wise to take a self-defense class, perhaps? Do you sleep around, but don't use protection? Increase safety measures wherever you can. Then, make a personal protective charm by tying up in a white cloth a pinch of salt, associated with protective solar energies. Carry the charm with you to help repel danger.

## Get Creative

Beltane has a very vibrant, creative, and fertile energy flow that can be utilized to help get your own creative projects off the ground. Ever thought about writing a book or a poem? Got an unfinished painting hiding out somewhere in the back of the closet? How about that hunk of art clay you never got around to using? Just as the seeds of the earth begin to sprout and grow, so too can ideas originating in the heart and mind find their way into the world of manifested reality come Beltane. It doesn't really matter what type of art you make. You might draw a picture, take some photos, make some music, choreograph a dance, crochet a hat, or even decorate a cake. As you make the art, envision your current wishes coming true, and do your best to allow yourself to actually feel and experience what it will feel like when that happens. Let this energy and emotion flow through your body and into the art. You'll have a Beltane masterpiece in no time that will remind you that you, too, are a creative spirit, just as is the sweet Mother Earth.

## *Enjoy Nature*

As with all the sabbats, Beltane marks a point in the year when it's especially beneficial to renew and strengthen our connection to Nature. It's a good day to tend to the outdoors, perhaps weeding, pruning, watering, or fertilizing. Consider planting some flowers or some vegetable seeds; perhaps plant a tree. Take a nature walk, or enjoy a picnic in a local park. Whatever you do outdoors, notice the plants, the sounds, the scents, and the sensations. Touch the vegetation. Enjoy the feel of sunshine on your skin. Observe, and see yourself as an integral and beautiful part of it all. If you can't get outdoors, get close to some houseplants, gently stroking their foliage or watering them while you think about how the plant lives and grows thanks to the cooperation between the sun, the water, the plant, and the soil. If you don't have houseplants, gaze out a window and take in as much as you can. Close your eyes and see what you can remember about what you see, hear, or sense. What can you imagine lies beyond your view? Envision it as clearly as possible, and imagine yourself out and about in this wild of your own creation.

## *Get Spiffy*

To the Celts, Beltane was a time of purification, when impurities and baneful influences were driven away from the people, their animals, their land, their possessions, and their homes. It's no coincidence that many modern Pagans see Beltane as a time of purification, too. The threat of winter having finally passed, it only makes sense that we also have an instinct to mimic Nature by shaking off the last remnants of lingering darkness and danger. We may find we get an urge to spruce up both ourselves and our homes, livening things up with a springtime makeover. Ritual baths, fire rituals, house smudging, and other methods are commonly employed at Beltane as a means of banishing negative energies and baneful influences.

For a purifying Beltane ritual bath, sea salt, lavender, or other purifying minerals and herbs might be placed in the bath water, as the practitioner visualizes any physical or spiritual impurities flowing out of the body and into the water. After the ritual bath, treat yourself to a spiffy springtime outfit and a new haircut or style, and you'll quickly feel renewed, refreshed, and in tune with Beltane's fertile, vibrant, and thriving energy flow.

Fire rituals might involve candles or campfires, with rites requiring participants to circle the fire or (carefully!) jump over the flames as a means of purifying mind, body, and spirit.

Clearing clutter and removing dust in the home can do wonders to banish the blues, while a vase of fresh flowers will energize your living space and remind you of Nature's beauty. As an additional purifying measure, sage may be lit and used to fumigate the home as well as one's ritual space and magickal tools, the action believed to chase away unwanted influences and clear out stagnant energies. Salt water or a mist of lavender essential oil and spring water can be used in place of the sage. Just spritz the perimeter of each room, beginning in the east and proceeding clockwise around the space.

## Go Crazy

Beltane is an excellent time for adventure, and rash, bold, spontaneous behavior is widely embraced. You might celebrate with an impromptu trip to an exotic locale, a short road trip to a neighboring town, or by finally mustering up the courage to hit on that special someone. Is there a sport you'd like to try, something daring? How about a new hobby, or a new class you'd like to take? Maybe there's a fear you're ready to face. Be daring, and embrace the fun and carefree spirit of Beltane. Doing so will empower you to make the most of the opportunities this exciting and dynamic time of year provides.

## Make Way to the Water

Wells, rivers, lakes, and other sacred water sources are often visited at Beltane as a way to honor the earth's fertility. Symbolic of femininity, life, creativity, and goddess energies, water is a perfect accompaniment to many Beltane proceedings, with rituals and picnics often held near large bodies of water and offerings placed near holy wells and sacred springs. Consider making a trip to a water source this Beltane, taking time to admire the beauty of the water, make a wish, and leave behind a gift or two. Just make sure the gift isn't a source of pollution; natural items like rocks or flowers, or small amounts of birdseed, fruit, or vegetables are all appropriate choices for Beltane offerings.

SPELLS
AND
DIVINATION

dance, growth, passion, love, union, cooperation, fertility, fairy

tection, purification, manifestation, handfastings, building sacred

visiting sacred wells, giving offerings, working with fairies, ritual

lking the boundaries of one's property, protecting plants, divin

nimals, people, and possessions astronomical midpoint, and sum

the spring equinox and summer solstice: Sun at 15 degrees of

n the northern hemisphere, Sun at 15 degrees of Scorpio in

uthern hemisphere. Female: Maiden Goddess, Mother Godde

Earth Goddess, water plants or animals, the Lover preparin

with her beloved Flora, Danu, Freyja, Maia, Shasti, Pros

Chin-hua fu-jen, Venus, Diana, Artemis, Aphrodite, Astart

ona, Rauni, Sarasvati, Horae, Pan, Cernunnos, Beal, Bala

Pluto Wotan, Odin, Oak King, Apollo, Ra, Mugwort Lu

ertility, protection, divination, communication, with spirits ener

purification, joy, love, prophetic dreams, renewal energy, vitality

wealth, fairy magick, luck success, strength Rose, Frankincens

asmine, Lemon, Pine, Mint visiting sacred wells, giving offe

airies, abundance, growth, passion, love, union, cooperation, ferti

tection, purification, manifestation, handfastings, building sacred

$\mathcal{B}$ELTANE HAS A strong, sensual, fertile, and swift-moving energy flow, making it an ideal time for spellwork and divination focused on love, romance, energy, purification, protection, manifestation, and abundance. Here are a few spells and divination methods to try this Beltane. Each technique can be easily customized to your unique needs and desires; just keep an open mind and trust in your own instincts, intuition, and powers of magick.

## Beltane Spells

As you work these spells, keep in mind that the heart of magick lies in the witch and not in the method. While spell instructions generally focus on outlining the particulars of the rite's outward form, the inner alchemy that takes place in the mind and heart of the witch is often glossed over or omitted entirely. Here, you'll find information about the inner magickal process that accompanies each working, but understand that this process will be experienced slightly differently by each individual witch.

Take these instructions as suggestions to guide you toward further developing your own magickal methods, and as indications of what you might expect during and after each spell. These spells can be used anytime, but they will be especially effective if worked on Beltane.

### Two as One Candle Spell for Love

This spell will help attract a partner for love and romance. You'll need two candles, two candleholders, a toothpick or needle or something else with which to scratch the wax, a fireproof dish, a bit of your own saliva, and matches or a lighter.

Find a special, quiet place to work this spell. Begin by clearing your head, letting your worries and mundane thoughts slip away. Sometimes this can be difficult if you have a lot on your mind. If that's the case, go ahead and take some time to think before trying to get into a mental state ready for magick. When you're able, clear your head and try to think of yourself as a magickal being, existing beyond ego, beyond identity and personality. Once your head is clear, next clear the space in which you'll be working the magick. Use visualization and willpower to mentally "push" any negative or stale energy out of the space. It can be helpful to walk in a circle as you use the palm of your hand or your wand to direct the unwanted energies out of the space. You should be able to sense the negative energy as you force it away from the area, and once you've banished it all, the space will have a clear, empty feeling.

It's now time to fill that clear space with powerful, desirable energies that can help you with your spell. Here, as in all magick, actually, the choice is entirely yours. Many witches begin by calling on the elements, inviting air, fire, water, and earth energies into the sacred space, then move on to invite the powers of Goddess and God to help with the magickal rite. You might want to call on specific entities or godforms that are closely associated with Beltane, such as Beal, the Horned God, or the Goddess in her Maiden aspect.

As you invite these forces into the space, be they elements or deities, focus on any identifying characteristics and *feel* the power of each energetic being as it enters the space. Remember that in the world of magick, the mind designs the plan, but the *emotions* are what enact it. If you're calling on the air element, for instance, feel the emotion that a fresh breeze brings you, use the incredible power of your own breath to connect with the elemental force that corresponds. Likewise, if you're calling on Goddess energies, conjure in your heart a mother's love, the love for one's mother, and your attachment to the earth and all it brings you and needs from you.

As you invite the elements, deities, or other powers, you'll want to do your best to *become* whatever energy or forces you are hoping will join you for your spellwork. Think about it, envision it, feel it, be it, and invite it to join you.

Now that the preliminaries are taken care of, it's time to get down to business. Hold one of the two candles in your hand and think about the kind of lover you want. Imagine the feeling you'll have when this new lover holds you, touches you, tells you how loved and attractive you are. Feel that, and focus on that feeling rather than on your need or desire for it. Say with determination and certainty, "This is not a candle, but my new lover that I hold." Light the candle and place it in a candleholder.

Now, hold the other candle in your hand and think about all your wonderful characteristics you have to offer your next romantic mate. Conjure in your heart and body a feeling of love and passion. Imagine that you are expressing your love and admiration for your new lover to come, and pour this energy into the candle in your hand. Use the toothpick to scratch your full name into the candle wax. Kiss the candle, and rub a bit of your own saliva down the length of it. Say with passion, "This is not a candle, but myself as a wonderful lover."

Pull the second lit candle out of the candleholder and light the candle and so that you'll have one in each hand, the candle representing yourself, and the candle representing your new lover to be. Use the candle flames to slightly melt the wax down one side of each candle, then press the two candles together so that they form a single candle with two wicks. Use the lighter to melt the bottom of the double candle a bit so that it will stick, then place it in the fireproof dish. Watch the flames burn as you imagine being with your new lover, and send feelings of love and passion into the double candle as it melts.

You can watch it burn all the way down, or put it out and light it again the next night and possibly the next, repeating the part where you pour love and passion into the double candle as it burns. Once the double candle has completely melted down, take the leftover lump of wax and place it in the sun on top of a large rock, preferably near a body of water if you have a nice place nearby. With luck and belief, you should find your next lover within the next three lunar cycles. While the spell is in effect, have faith in it, but try not to dwell on it too much or doubt it as this can inhibit the magick. Pay attention to the people you interact with, and be on the lookout for new faces and personalities that seem inexplicably drawn to you or in tune with you. Keep your mind, heart, and eyes open, and look and act your best to give the spell the greatest chance for success. If you're not satisfied with results after a few months have passed, repeat or try a different spell, approaching the magickal goal from another angle.

### Fast-Acting Loving Herbs Spell

Here's another love spell that's very simple, requiring nothing but a small scrap of pink cloth, a piece of red or purple string or ribbon, and a small handful of common herbs you can probably find in your cupboard, garden, or neighborhood. Herbs, like all living things, are each filled with their own energetic vibrations and attributes that can be activated and directed into magickal power. This spell incorporates several herbs that are especially effective in attracting love and romance, as well as an herb to help speed along the magick. Since the power behind the magick is in this case primarily in the herbs, this spell demands only minimal mental effort and emotional energy from the witch who casts it.

You'll need some rosemary (for love and general magickal power), some basil (for love), some rose petals (for love and romance), and a sprig of mint (for swiftness). Fresh herbs are more potent, but dried herbs will do in a pinch. Cut the pink or white fabric into a circle about five inches or so in diameter. Place the herbs one at a time on top of the cloth, thinking of each herb's attributes and conjuring the same sort of energy as you do so. For example, as you add the rose petals, think of love and romance and project the emotion of these energies into the herb. Once all the herbs are on the cloth, mix them all together with your fingertips or wand, stating as you do so that these herbs will bring love quickly. Pull up the edges of the fabric into a bundle, and use the string or ribbon to tie up the top and keep all the contents in place. Hold the bundle in your hand, close to your heart, and project into it a feeling of love. Carry it with you to attract new romance. Opportunities should start to manifest within a few days time. This charm is fast acting, but it isn't long lasting. After a couple of weeks, untie the bundle and cast the herbs to the wind, sending with it romantic wishes for all the lonely souls in the world who haven't yet found someone to love.

## Sun and Citrine Spell
## for Energy and Purification

Feeling sluggish and tired or like you're stuck in a mental rut? This spell utilizes the power of the sun and the natural power of salt and stones to clear away stagnation and give your body and mind a boost of energy for Beltane. You'll need salt, a small citrine crystal, and a sunny, outdoor place in which to work the spell. Begin by kneeling down and placing both of your palms flat down on the ground. Let yourself feel tired, sluggish, bored, wan—whatever it is that's ailing you. Allow these energies to flow freely through your body, then direct the flow out through your hands and into the bare ground. Empty your body of as much stale, sluggish energy as possible, letting it drain into the earth until you experience an empty, hollow sort of feeling. Next, take the salt and sprinkle it over the dirt into which you've just released your body's stale energy. Salt has a purifying quality that will help clear away the patterns going on behind the scenes of your current rut.

Now, turn your attention to the sun, and feel the warm sunlight as it shines on your skin. Focus on the warmth and brightness, and tell this energy to enter your body. Envision the light flowing into you, and feel the heat and the strength filling you up from top to bottom. You may want to raise your hands or your wand up toward the sun to help facilitate the energy flow.

Next, hold the citrine stone up to the sun. Citrine has many energetic attributes in common with sunlight. Like the sun, citrine has a strong, very positive vibration, and it's also great at neutralizing or purifying negativity and other forms of "darkness." As you hold the citrine skyward, use visualization and willpower to "pull" the sunlight into the stone. You should feel the stone "charging up," which you may sense as an increase in temperature or as a higher rate of energetic vibration. Once the stone feels "full," place it on top of the scattered salt. Rub the citrine over the surface of the area, moving the salt crystals around and thinking about how you're ready for something new, a boost of fresh energy to inspire you with fresh purpose and motivate you toward new adventure. Imagine as vividly as you can, so that you actually *feel* and experience emotionally what it will be like to have greater energy, to feel awake and powerful, to feel excited and renewed. Pay attention to your body posture and adjust it accordingly so that you're physically aligned with your goal. (For instance, if you want to feel happy, then stand like you're happy, smile like you're happy, etc.) Hold the citrine in your palm now, and sprinkle a bit more fresh salt over it. Rub it around in the salt on your palm as you let more sunlight pour into the mix. Feel the energy; sense the enormous power in the citrine increasing and vibrating wildly. Affirm out loud or mentally that, "Like the sun and this stone, I am supercharged and energized!"

The spell is complete. Carry the citrine with you or leave it in an open area of your home for best results. You should experience an immediate boost of energy that should continue for at least several days and possibly for much longer, depending on the strength of your magick in comparison to the strength of the energy-zapping factors you encounter in your daily life.

### Beltane Bean-Planting Spell
### for Manifestation and Abundance

This spell is reminiscent of a magickal act carried out during the Hopi *Powanu*, or Bean-Planting Ceremony. Shortly before the growing season, beans were planted indoors in containers meant to represent the larger fields outdoors that would soon bear the crops. These miniature indoor "crops" would be watered, tended to, prayed over, and cared for, and fires were lit in the home to help speed along the germination of the seeds. If the beans sprouted, it was taken as an indication that the larger, actual crops would also do well, and it was believed that the action of tending to the mini crops helped to ensure such success. Most of us don't grow crops, but we do grow other things in our lives. This spell incorporates aspects of the Hopi tradition into a more contemporary magickal working that's both relevant and effective for the modern witch. You'll need a handful of dried beans of any variety, some dirt, and a flowerpot, shallow pan, or other container in which to plant the beans. You'll also need a few pieces of quartz crystal and several candles colored white, gold, or yellow.

Begin by filling the container with soil. It's best to avoid potted plant mixtures that contain chemical fertilizers, but try to find a nice quality soil to give your spell optimal conditions. Think of the earth and the growing things, the plants and the trees, the animals and other living creatures that inhabit the planet. Feel how you *are* one of these living creatures, just another of the growing things living on Earth. Think about how our lives are linked to and dependent on the earth: the earth provides both the foundation and the fuel on which we grow. Although you only have before you a small container of earth, it is energetically one in the same as the greater earth outside your door. Place your hands over the container and affirm out loud or to yourself, "This is the earth. This is the place where my wishes become manifest. This is the land in which I will grow."

Envision the entire planet, seeing your place on the globe as you stand right where you are.

Now, think of flourishing plants all over the world, imagining their appearance and smells as clearly as possible. Hold the beans in your hand and think about how those particular seeds will also flourish. For each bean, envision one of your goals manifesting. Imagine that you've already got what you want, and project the emotion and feeling that gives you into each respective "wish bean" you prepare. Plant the beans in the container of dirt and pour some water over it. Poke the bottom ends of the quartz crystals into the soil so that the points stick out a bit. Quartz is a natural amplifier of energy, and its presence will help magnify the magickal power you've already poured into the wish beans.

Surround the container with the candles, thinking as you do so of the sun and its intense power that fuels the earth. Light the candles, inviting the sunlight and any other energies or entities you like to enter the flames, lending their strength to help your wish beans thrive. Think of the power of the candle flames, the power of the sun, flowing into the beans and into your wishes, charging them up to grow. Extinguish the candles to close this part of the working.

The spell is not yet complete. You'll need to continue to water and care for your wish beans until they sprout. Sit beside the container for a few minutes each day and send a feeling of love and joy down into the soil and into the beans. Envision all your wishes as manifest, imagining total success in all your endeavors. Repeat each day until the beans sprout, then keep them or transfer them to an outdoor location if desired. The sprouting of the beans should coincide with the time when each wish begins to manifest in earnest. If many of your wish beans fail to sprout, you might want to reexamine those particular corresponding wishes, or else blame it on the soil quality and simply try again!

## Beltane Divination

Like the spells above, these divination methods can be worked anytime, but they may be more effective if used on or around Beltane. Keep in mind that any divination system, whether a complex tool like the tarot or something as simple as a daisy blossom, acts as a tool and a doorway only, allowing you easier access to the collective consciousness and to your own inner intuition and psychic abilities. Trust your senses, and be open to the information and feelings that come to you.

### *Fortunetelling with Eggs and Bannocks*

One traditional fortunetelling method practiced on Beltane in Scotland, England, and elsewhere involved rolling certain foodstuffs down hills. Hard-boiled eggs and/or bannocks, a type of thick, round oatmeal cake with one side marked with a cross, were taken to the top of a hill and rolled down the side. The fate of the egg or bannock as it reached the end of the hill was taken as an indication of the fate of the one who rolled it—if the egg remained intact, and if the bannock landed blank-side up, it signified good fortune, whereas if the eggshell cracked or the bannock landed cross-side up, it indicated that poor luck was to be expected. Here's a modern variation of this traditional folk divination method; try it with friends for maximum fun.

Boil some eggs, and if you don't want to bother searching for a traditional bannock recipe, simply bake up a batch of biscuits. On each of the eggs, write a goal, wish, or question for which you would like to know the prospects. On each of the biscuits, draw a solar symbol on either the top or bottom surface. Take the biscuits and eggs to a grassy hill and roll them down, thinking of the goal, wish, or question with each one as you release it down the hill. If an eggshell should crack, or a biscuit lands solar-symbol up, interpret it as an answer of no, unlikely, or not at this time. On the other hand, if the egg travels downhill unscathed, or the biscuit lands solar-symbol downward, it's interpreted as an answer of yes, a sign of good fortune, and an affirmation that your goals and wishes will likely come true.

### Flower Fortune

Here's a traditional Beltane divination custom that's extremely simple. Go out into a field of daisies or dandelions, close your eyes, and pick a large handful while thinking of an important long-term goal. Traditionally, the goal was typically marriage, but you can adapt this method to discern the fate of any ambition. Open your eyes and count the total number of flower blossoms in your bouquet. The number indicates how many years will pass before your wish comes true. As an alternative, you can ask a yes or no question as you pick the flowers, then determine the answer by counting the number of blossoms— an even number indicates a no, while an odd number of flowers signifies a yes.

## Love Match Tarot Divination

This divination method can help you identify a potential love match for Beltane or beyond. Begin by separating out the court cards, which includes the page, the knight, the queen, and the king of each suit. If you like, you can also take out the magician, the high priestess, the empress, the emperor, the hierophant, the hermit, the hanged man, the devil, and the fool. All these cards represent specific archetypes and personality traits. You can omit the major arcana cards if you like, but it gives you a broader sampling and symbolic representation of the general populace if you include the complete set of archetypal cards, which should number twenty-five in total.

Next, turn your focus to the remaining cards of the deck. Look through them one by one, selecting any cards that appear to you to represent elements you'd like to have in a future relationship, ways in which you hope your new partner will shine. Don't go by the card meanings listed in a book; rather, use your own intuition and emotional response to gauge the significance of each image.

Once you've selected as many cards as you like, spread these out before you, face up. Beneath them, place the twenty-five archetypal cards face down. You can place them in a big pile, line them up in a single row, or arrange them in five rows of five. Look again at the cards you have face up and think about the aspects you hope to find in your next romance. Concentrate on the question "Who will give it to me?" and, without peeking, select from the twenty-five archetypal cards. The card you select is an indication of the sort of person that would be ideally suited for you as a romantic partner.

While traditionally the court cards are gender-associated and color-based (the page as male or female, queens as female, knights and kings as male, cups as fair-skinned, fair-haired people, pentacles as dark-skinned, dark-haired people, and so on), there's no need to restrict your interpretations to these outdated guidelines. As previously mentioned, these cards represent archetypes and personality traits, which can appear in anyone, regardless of gender, hair, and skin color, etc.

The archetypal cards *can*, however, give an accurate indication of maturity level, which often, but not always, corresponds with age. A king or queen or archetypal card of the major arcana (empress, emperor, etc.) tends to be more mature and serious-minded, more set in their ways than a less experienced and playful page, while a knight is usually of an adult maturity level but still energetic and youthful in many ways.

Examine the other attributes revealed in the card you've selected for further clues about your best potential love match. What personality traits does the card represent? Is a specific occupation or station in life indicated by the card's name, imagery, or symbolism? Consult tarot guides for detailed card meanings, follow your own intuition, or utilize the interpretations for the court cards provided below to help you identify your ideal partner:

**Page of Cups:** Be on the lookout for someone very youthful and playful, with a fun-loving, artistic, live-for-the-moment spirit. They may be lacking in practicality and planning, but they make up for it in enthusiasm and spontaneity.

**Knight of Cups:** Drawing this card signifies you belong with someone very romantic, the type likely to declare their affections in elaborate, dramatic ways. This type knows how to express affection and admiration and does so freely.

**Queen of Cups:** Look for someone with a kind, loving, romantic heart, but who keeps their most inner self rather hidden. This type tends to appear very light, bubbly, and outgoing in spirit, though they usually have a more secretive side where their deepest affections and passions are kept concealed from all but those deemed most worthy.

**King of Cups:** If you choose this card, it indicates that you would be happy with a partner who is joyful, compassionate, caring, and loving. This person will be self-assured and confident, though generally soft-spoken. Their heart rules over their head, and they tend to be very sentimental and usually have a good sense of humor and a very strong love of laughter, friends, and family.

**Page of Wands:** This card reveals that a partner who is youthful, loyal, and an excellent communicator would be great for you. In another sense, this card might point to a person whose profession involves communications or making deliveries.

**Knight of Wands:** If you choose this card, keep your eyes open for someone very unconventional and different. This type loves to impress and they hold in high esteem those who will listen to their ideas, which can sometimes be a bit far-fetched or idealistic. This person may be a little egotistical or conceited, but they live life to the beat of their own drum and are decidedly nonconformist, refusing to be restricted by convention, tradition, or societal and cultural norms.

**Queen of Wands:** This is a person who is independent, confident, and much bolder than they may appear to most people. They typically have a strong love for animals and nature. They tend to be very social, and they enjoy a good party. Their affections are rather changeable, but on the bright side, they rarely have trouble letting go of negative circumstances and people. This type is often self-made, rising from a lower station in life to achieve greater success through one's own talent, ambition, and effort.

**King of Wands:** This card indicates a person who is successful, established, respected, and unconventional. They tend to live "in their own little world," and may have trouble seeing other people's perspectives. This type can come across as domineering, but it's often just how their insecurity finds its way to the surface.

**Page of Pentacles:** Be on the lookout for a serious-minded, youthful individual. This type has excellent focus, and they are usually hard workers and dedicated students. If you pick this card, the partner you'd like best might very well be a student or a person who has just recently entered the world of employment and is eager to advance in their profession. This type can be a bit dull and boring at times, but they're sensible, practical, intelligent, and responsible.

**Knight of Pentacles:** This is a person who is practical and sensible. They enjoy the simple things in life, and they don't mind working hard in order to make that possible. They are dedicated and determined and can sometimes be a little too single-minded in perception and purpose. This type usually has a love for animals and a strong appreciation for the natural world.

**Queen of Pentacles:** Keep your eyes open for a person who is strongly independent, passionate, and earthy. They tend to be a bit on the introverted side, and they love very deeply. This type tends to act too clingy at times and can have trouble letting go, but on the plus side, they're very loyal and practical, and they'll be there for you when you need them.

**King of Pentacles:** Drawing this card reveals you might be suited to a partner who is mature, established, and wealthy. This type often has great success in business enterprises and agricultural endeavors, as they usually have both good mathematical skill as well as a green thumb. They love the finer things in life and they place great value and importance on luxury and material wealth, but they are also earthy in spirit with a strong connection to nature and a healthy appreciation for the beauty of the natural world. They often enjoy providing for the comfort and needs of the people around them.

**Page of Swords:** This person is bold, rash, and a bit of a rebel. They often have the attitude of someone with something to prove, and they can be rather irresponsible and unscrupulous at times, pursuing personal goals with little regard for consequences. This type can be dishonest at times, but on the positive side, they live for the moment and they love to take chances and make stuff happen. This is a person of action and bravery, with a heavy dose of cockiness.

**Knight of Swords:** If you draw this card, be on the lookout for the heroic type. This is an individual who is brave, bold, and the champion of noble causes. They strive to do the right thing at all costs, regardless of the amount of effort or sacrifice required. This trait can make them appear a little single-minded at times, as they tend to put causes and principles before people. This person will likely be extremely charming, energetic, and strong in spirit and personality, a real "knight in shining armor" type.

**Queen of Swords:** This card indicates a person who is strong, determined, graceful, and tenacious. They tend to have a commanding personality and they fit well in leadership roles. This type appears to have everything together at all times, maintaining an austere countenance regardless of any inner turmoil that might be happening. They tend to have a touch of inner sadness that they try very hard to conceal, as they place high importance on keeping up an appearance of normalcy. They're often misunderstood as being "cold," but once you melt the ice, they love very deeply and often forever. They will stand up for the people they believe in and cherish regardless of circumstances or the opinions of others.

**King of Swords:** If you draw this card, it may be that an individual with a very forceful personality and commanding presence would suit you best. This type is often in positions of power and leadership. They can have strong tempers and often develop bossy attitudes and behaviors. They usually feel most comfortable when playing a dominant role in their personal relationships. They have great determination, and once dedicated to any particular pursuit, idea, or course of action, they're very unlikely to change paths or switch positions.

# RECIPES
# AND
# CRAFTS

dance, growth, passion, love, union, cooperation, fertility faery
tection, purification, manifestation, handfastings, building sacred
visiting sacred wells, giving offerings, working with faeries, ritual
lking the boundaries of one's property, protecting plants, divine
nimals, people, and possessions astronomical midpoint, and sun
the spring equinox and summer solstice: Sun at 15 degrees of
n the northern hemisphere, Sun at 15 degrees of Scorpio in t
uthern hemisphere. Female: Maiden Goddess, Mother Godde
Earth Goddess, water plants or animals, the Lover preparing
with her beloved Flora, Danu, Freyja, Maia, Shasti, Pros
Chin-hua fu-jen, Venus, Diana, Artemis, Aphrodite, Istar
ona, Rauni, Sarasvati, Horae, Pan, Cernunnos, Beal, Bald
Pluto Wotan, Odin, Oak King, Apollo, Ra, Mugwort Le
ertility, protection, divination, communication, with spirits energy
urification, joy, love, prophetic dreams, renewal energy, vitality
wealth, fairy magick, luck success, strength Rose, Frankincense
smine, Lemon, Pine, Mint visiting sacred wells, giving offe
ces, abundance, growth, passion, love, union, cooperation, fertil
tion, purification, manifestation, handfastings, building social

$\mathcal{W}$HILE RITUALS, DIVINATION, and spellwork are indeed awesome ways to celebrate the sabbats, we sometimes overlook the simpler ways that can be just as fulfilling and meaningful. When we incorporate the practice of the sabbats into our non-ritual lives as well, we gain greater satisfaction and a deeper understanding of the energetic changes that come with each of the eight sacred days. In this chapter, you'll find ideas for recipes, crafts, and decor to help you celebrate Beltane in practical, anyone-can-do-it ways that will have you feeling like you are living your craft and walking the walk of a true witch, not just in ritual but in everyday mundane life, too.

## Beltane Recipes

Beltane is a great time for get-togethers, and nothing gets people together more quickly than some delicious culinary fare. As summer begins to stir and temperatures continue to rise, many modern Pagans find it's the perfect time to enjoy a meal outdoors in the sunshine. Consider hosting a picnic or a barbecue, and keep foods on the light side to harmonize with Beltane's bright, quick-moving energies. Fruits, vegetables, and light pastries can be swiftly converted by the body into energy you can put into your Beltane magick, whereas heavy foods, such as fatty meats and thick gravies, have a slower vibration that can make you sluggish.

Here's a breakfast picnic featuring light, tasty fare just right for Beltane. Each recipe is designed with ingredients chosen for their magickal attributes, and instructions are included for adding magickal intention to the cooking process. Feel free to adapt these recipes to suit your own personal taste and style.

### *Blessed Lemon Custard*

This delicious lemon custard is magickally crafted to express gratitude for your Beltane blessings while manifesting even more blessings.

*Ingredients:*

4 cups milk

⅔ cup sugar

4 whole eggs and 2 egg yolks (6 eggs total, two separated)

4 tablespoons lemon juice

1 teaspoon vanilla extract

Graham crackers

1 tablespoon powdered sugar (optional)

1 sprig fresh mint (optional)

Begin by heating milk in a saucepan over medium heat until it begins to steam and bubble slightly (and *before* it begins to scald or boil). Add in sugar and stir till dissolved. Add eggs. (To separate an egg, just crack the shell and pour the contents of the egg back and forth between the two shell halves, letting the egg white drip into a bowl until you have only the yolk remaining.) Stir slowly with a wooden spoon until the mixture is thoroughly blended. You may need to reduce the heat slightly; you want it to bubble gently, but never quite come to a rolling boil. If it starts to boil over, lift the pot off the burner and allow it to cool for a few seconds. Continue to stir frequently, using slow, gentle motions. As the mixture continues to heat, it will begin to noticeably thicken. This might take as long as 15 minutes, so be patient and don't take your eyes off it.

Once the custard looks visibly different, and much more puddinglike, reduce the heat slightly and let the custard continue to cook for about another 5 minutes.

Custard can be tricky, and sometimes it doesn't seem to want to thicken no matter how long you cook it. If you experience this problem, never fear. Just slowly sprinkle in a few tablespoons of flour, adding in a little at a time and whisking the custard very briskly to help remove any lumps. The end result is technically a pastry cream and not a custard, and the texture will be a bit different, but it will still taste delicious.

Once the custard has thickened to your satisfaction, remove it from heat, then stir in the lemon juice and vanilla extract. As you put in the lemon juice, think of the sunlight and moonlight. As you put in the vanilla extract, which has an energetic vibration in tune with love and romance, think of the love between the Goddess and the God, nature, and humankind and individual. Pour the custard into a bowl, let it cool to room temperature, then refrigerate until cold.

Next, place graham cracker pieces on the bottom and sides of individual serving dishes as you think about the solid earth, Mother Nature's womb from which springs the bounty of May flowers, fruits, and greenery. Fill each dish with the lemon custard as you think about the beautiful, blossoming earth and contemplate all the delights you hope Beltane will bring. Garnish with a light sprinkle of powdered sugar and a sprig of fresh mint if desired.

## Abundance Berries with Cream

This creation will help manifest an abundance of romance or whatever else you'd like this Beltane.

*Ingredients:*
1 pound mixed fresh berries
1 cup heavy whipping cream
2 tablespoons honey

Start with a batch of mixed fresh berries. Strawberries and raspberries have a loving, passionate energy that's especially good for conjuring up romantic fun, but any type of berry can be attuned to your specific aim and used effectively in this recipe. Wash the berries, drain thoroughly, then place them in an attractive bowl, thinking of your magickal goal. For the cream, pour cold heavy whipping cream into a chilled bowl. For best results, use a metal bowl and metal whisk, placing them in the refrigerator or freezer beforehand to get them very cold. Make sure the bowl and whisk are dry and free of any moisture or condensation before you begin. Whip the cream with the whisk until it starts to thicken, then slowly drizzle in honey.

As you work the mixture, think of the fertility of the earth and the animals, the archetypal mother and the "milk" she provides to her children. Continue to whip the cream until it reaches the desired consistency. Turn your thoughts to abundance and manifestation as the cream begins to solidify. You'll know it's ready when you see soft peaks forming in the cream, or when it no longer drips easily off a spoon. To save time, you can mix the cream with an electric mixer, but it can be a much more rewarding and magickal experience when accomplished the old-fashioned way. Serve the berries in small bowls, garnishing each dish with a dollop of the whipped cream. For a fancier-looking treat, serve the berries and cream in a clear crystal goblet or wine glass, making repeating layers of berries, cream, berries, cream, and so on.

### Honey Wishing Yogurt

This simple yogurt dish is especially blended to help Beltane wishes come true.

*Ingredients:*
4 cups vanilla yogurt
¼ cup honey
Graham crackers, bran cereal, or fresh apple slices (optional)

Start with vanilla yogurt, add in honey, and stir as you focus on happy wishes. Think of something that makes you feel extremely good, then project this feeling of joy into the yogurt mixture. Serve with graham crackers or garnish with bran cereal if desired. If you like, have your guests dip their apple slices in the yogurt, make a wish, then take a bite.

## Vanilla Cinnamon Thrill Iced Coffee

This cold coffee drink is designed to increase feelings of excitement, pleasure, love, and passion in all who drink it.

*Ingredients:*
1 pot of brewed coffee
1 teaspoon cinnamon
2 to 3 teaspoons vanilla extract
Milk, half-and-half, or sugar to taste (optional)

Make a pot of coffee (medium or light roast works best) the night before your picnic. As the coffee heats, envision the coffee beans growing in the strong sunlight, and think of the tremendous amount of warmth and energy the sun provides. Once the coffee is brewed, stir in cinnamon, thinking as you do so of cinnamon's hot, passionate energy. Daydream of something that excites you as you let the coffee cool to room temperature, then leave it in the refrigerator overnight. In the morning, add vanilla extract and project a feeling of love and pleasure into the coffee as you stir. Serve over ice, mixing in sugar and milk or half-and-half to taste. If you know all your guests will want sweet coffee, add the sugar before cooling the coffee, as it will dissolve much better that way. Otherwise, just stir it very briskly until its blended to your satisfaction.

# Beltane Barbecue

Here's a menu for a Beltane barbecue. As with the breakfast picnic, each recipe is designed with ingredients chosen for their magickal attributes. The instructions include tips for adding magickal intention to the cooking process. Feel free to adapt these recipes to suit your own personal taste and style.

### Grilled Portobelo Mushroom Beltane Tune-Up Burgers

These vegetarian "burgers" will help you attune with Beltane's magickal energies.

*Ingredients:*
Portobelo mushrooms, one per serving
Olive oil
Sea salt
Buns
Lettuce, tomatoes, onions, mayonnaise, mustard, ketchup, and other condiments as desired

Wash the mushrooms, removing the stems but leaving the caps intact. Notice the mushroom's natural shape, which many cultures consider to be a sacred symbol of the gods and also a phallic symbol, resembling the male genitalia. Think of the masculine, solar energies gaining strength at Beltane as you gently pat the mushrooms dry. Next, brush the mushrooms with a light coating of olive oil, a symbol of love. As you do so, think of the love and romance you hope Beltane will bring to you. Sprinkle the mushrooms with a pinch of sea salt, associated with purification and divine feminine power. Contemplate the mingling of feminine and masculine energies as you sprinkle the salt, and envision any negativity or rigid obstacles in your life dissolving. Place the mushrooms on the hot grill, turning once every few minutes until both sides are tender. This can take anywhere from 5 to 10 minutes, depending on the hotness of the grill and the thickness of the mushrooms. You'll know when they're ready because you'll notice an obvious change in color and smell. Serve it on a toasted bun like a hamburger, and top with lettuce, tomatoes, onions, mayonnaise, mustard, ketchup, and any other desired condiments.

## Sexy Rosemary and Garlic-Roasted Asparagus

This simple recipe will help you feel empowered and sensual, confident and sexy and ready for some Beltane romance.

*Ingredients:*
1 pound fresh, whole asparagus
1 tablespoon butter
1 clove garlic, minced
¼ teaspoon salt
1 sprig fresh rosemary

Start with whole, fresh asparagus, thoroughly washed and patted dry. Place the asparagus in the center of a medium-sized piece of aluminum foil, lining the stems up side by side so that all the tips are facing the same way. Notice how the asparagus mimics the shape of the priapic, or pinecone-tipped wand, a magickal implement associated with Dionysus, god of forests, pleasure, lust, and wine, and a manifestation of the divine masculine in one of its more lusty forms. Place a small pat of butter on top of the asparagus; sprinkle the garlic evenly over the asparagus. Season with the salt. Place a sprig of fresh rosemary on top of the asparagus as you envision laying a kiss on someone you admire. Fold the sides of the foil so that the asparagus is completely covered, then place the bundle on the grill for about 10 minutes. Think of the symbolic rising of the god force both within the blossoming earth and within yourself as the asparagus heats.

## Friendly Rainbow Pasta Salad

This easy Beltane side dish is designed to increase feelings of friendship and community. Make this ahead of time so that when your grilling is done, you can just pull it out of the refrigerator ready to serve.

*Ingredients:*
1 pound rainbow rotini
1 teaspoon olive oil
⅔ cup ranch salad dressing
½ cup chopped black olives
¼ teaspoon salt
¼ cup Parmesan cheese

Bring a large pot of water to a boil, then add one pound of dried rainbow rotini and a pinch of salt. Notice the different colors of pasta, and think about how people of all ages and colors and dispositions come together to enjoy the May sunshine. Think of your friends and send your good feelings into the rotini as it cooks. Boil until the pasta is al dente, about 8 minutes. Drain the pasta and rinse it with cold water. Drizzle olive oil over the pasta, envisioning a loving, compassionate energy raining down upon the people of your community. Gently toss the pasta until the oil is evenly distributed. Allow the rotini to cool to room temperature, then place it in the refrigerator until it's thoroughly cold. Add the ranch salad dressing, chopped black olives, salt, and Parmesan cheese. When you add the olives, think again of love, friendship, and compassion. Mix thoroughly, then store cold until you're ready to eat.

## Supercharged Sun Cakes

These light and yummy cookies will increase your energy and help you attune with Beltane's strong solar vibrations.

*Ingredients:*
2 cups all-purpose flour
1 cup sugar
¼ teaspoon salt
1 teaspoon baking powder
¼ teaspoon baking soda
2 sticks butter, softened
1 egg
¼ cup orange juice
2 teaspoons grated orange zest

Preheat oven to 350°F. Mix together flour, sugar, salt, baking powder, and baking soda. Blend in softened butter, then add egg. Citrus is associated with solar energies, so your sun cakes will need a touch of orange flavoring to be complete. Stir in orange juice and grated orange zest, inviting the powers of the sun to enter into the mix. Let the dough chill, then roll tablespoon-sized pieces into small balls, place on a greased cookie sheet about an inch apart, and flatten slightly. Bake for about 10 minutes.

## Come Together Lemonade

This magickal lemonade can help facilitate cooperation and feelings of togetherness and camaraderie. As a citrus fruit, lemons are associated with the sun, but their more subtle vibrations associate the fruit with lunar goddess energies as well, making them an especially suitable choice for a Beltane beverage base symbolic of the union between the Goddess and the God.

*Ingredients:*
9 lemons
1 gallon cold water
2 cups sugar

Cut lemons in half horizontally, then score the cut sides and squeeze out the juice. As you squeeze the juice from the lemons, contemplate the gifts that nature gives to us, the tremendous amount of energy poured into the earth by the Goddess and the God in order to make it bloom. Add the lemon juice to a gallon of cold water, then stir in sugar. Project your own feelings of love and gratitude into the lemonade as you stir in the sugar. Add a bit more sugar if it's not as sweet as you like. Serve over ice and enjoy.

## Magickal May Wine

Drink this May wine to welcome in the spring and renew your sense of youth and vigor. Substitute sparkling white grape juice or apple cider for the white wine to make a nonalcoholic version.

*Ingredients:*

7 to 10 sprigs fresh woodruff, flowers removed

One piece of string, about 8 inches long

1 bottle white wine (preferably a young wine, from the previous year's vintage)

2 tablespoons honey (optional)

1 16-ounce bottle club soda (optional)

Extra woodruff sprigs or leaves (for optional garnish)

Several fresh strawberries (for optional garnish)

One small orange, thinly sliced (for optional garnish)

Begin by tying the stems of the woodruff together with the length of string, creating a bundle. As you prepare the woodruff, think about the plant's energy, associated with sexuality, protection, and magickal power. Open the white wine and tuck the bundle of woodruff into the bottle so that the herbs are submerged in the liquid, and the length of string hangs out the top of the bottleneck. Let this sit for a couple of hours, then pull the woodruff out of the bottle. Chill the wine in the refrigerator.

If you want to make a sweet wine, drizzle honey into the wine bottle, put the cork back in, and shake it around a bit until the honey blends with the wine. Your May wine is ready to drink at this point, but if you prefer to jazz it up a bit, pour the wine into a large punch bowl, add the club soda, and toss in a few orange slices and woodruff leaf clusters to float on the surface of the liquid. If you like, garnish each individual serving with a fresh strawberry cut with a slit at the bottom so that it can be placed along the rim of the wine glass.

# Beltane Crafts

While rituals, spells, and meditations help us connect with the deeper meaning of each sabbat, there's nothing like some hands-on practical crafting to help us get in sync with the energetic flow of the season. Here are some easy-to-make crafts to create this Beltane.

## A Priapic Wand

A priapic (pinecone-tipped) wand is an ideal tool for Beltane magick and a perfect symbol of the season. With a young pinecone at its tip, the wand is symbolic of fertility and sexuality. The pinecone's shape is reminiscent of a phallus, and is thus considered a sacred emblem of deity in its masculine, young, and lusty form. Why not make your own priapic wand this Beltane? A priapic wand is great for use in love spells and lust magick, and it will also bring a boost of extra confidence, energy, and strength to all your magickal workings.

*You will need:*

One stick: straight, between 9 and 13 inches, forked or cleaved
    end if possible and desired

One young pinecone: preferably of the young, green variety,
    and with a narrow base or stem on the end

Gloves

String or yarn: preferably green, pink, or yellow

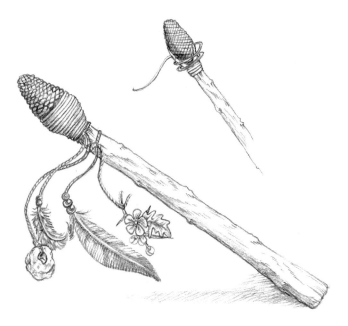

Pocketknife (optional)

Sand paper, nail file, or rough rock (optional)

Other trimmings such as flowers, leaves, or feathers (optional)

To get started, you'll need to first find a stick to use for the wand. Please do choose from fallen sticks rather than breaking limbs off of a living tree. Try to find a stick that is fairly straight and wand-length—which is a matter of opinion, but generally falls in the nine to thirteen inch range, varying according to individual beliefs, traditions, and preferences. Willow, oak, pine, or hawthorn are especially good choices, but let your intuition take precedence over specific wood type. If you're not comfortable working with a pocketknife, try to find a stick with a natural split or fork at one of the ends.

You'll also need to find a pinecone to use for the wand tip. The green, freshly budded stage is what you want, preferably with a narrow base and/or a small stem piece on the bottom so that it's easier to attach to the wand.

Once you've gathered your supplies, begin by preparing the stick, removing loose dirt and bark if desired, and breaking off any extraneous twigs. Use sandpaper, a rough rock, or a nail file to smooth down any sharp places. If you've chosen a stick that has neither a forked end nor a natural cleave in the end, you'll have to make some adjustments. Put on your protective gloves and use a pocketknife to cut a small slit vertically down through the middle of the wand tip, about a half inch to one inch deep. Wedge the base of the pinecone into the slit or between the forks at the wand tip.

Use string or yarn to secure the pinecone in place. Just cut off a piece of string around twelve inches long, then tie the end of the string around the wand near the base of the pinecone, making a secure knot. Then wrap the string around the wand

and continue wrapping until you've covered about a third of the pinecone. Tuck in the end of the string and tie to secure.

Your priapic wand is essentially now ready, but if you like, you can jazz it up a bit. Consider adding ornamentation such as flowers, leaves, beads, or feathers, securing them with string. More perishable additions, including the leaves and flowers, can be added at the last minute right before ritual so that they'll still be fresh when it's time for magick.

Once you're happy with the general design, take a moment to empower your wand, charging it up and expressing your intention for the wand to be a tool of magick. You can do so by simply holding the wand skyward toward the sun, and inviting any elemental forces or deities you like to work with to enter the wand. For example, you might say something like:

> *Into this wand, I welcome the power of the sun,*
> *the strength of the earth,*
> *the magick of the gods.*
> *Serve me well and I will serve the world*
> *with love and light and magick.*

Use your priapic wand for love magick; passion or lust-inducing spellwork; magick to increase strength, courage, or energy; and any other Beltane rites you feel called to do.

## Beltane Floral Crown

As symbols of fertility, life, and beauty, flowers are a prominent element in many springtime traditions. In ancient Rome, the goddess Flora was often depicted wearing a ring of flowers around her head, while the May Queen of European May Day celebrations donned similar attire. If you'd like to add some festive flair to your Beltane fashions this year, consider crafting a floral crown of your own to wear. This design doubles as a decorative wreath.

*You will need:*
6 vines, thin and pliable sticks, or long and thick grasses or
flower stems: each about 2 to 2.5 feet long
Flowers
String
Scissors and/or garden shears

Begin by gathering all your supplies. You'll need to first find enough vines or other materials to make the basic wreath. Ideally, you want vines that are brown on the outside, but still green on the inside. If you can't find that, though, you can use thin, pliable sticks, long and thick grasses, or extra long and sturdy flower stems instead. If you're planning to wear the wreath as a crown, measure the materials as you gather them to make sure it will be large enough to fit around your head. You'll need about six strands of vines or whatever else you're using, cut to a length of around two to two and a half feet.

You'll also need to find some flowers to decorate your Beltane wreath. Use whatever you can find growing near your home, or visit a florist and ask for local, seasonal blossoms. Keep the flowers in water so they'll stay fresh until you're ready to begin.

Start by laying out the long strands for the wreath, placing the vines, sticks, stems, or grasses side by side. If your materials don't seem flexible enough, soak them in water for a couple of hours to make them more pliable. Cut a piece of string about four inches long, and use this to tie the strands together at one end. Leave the excess string in place.

Separate the strands into three sets of pairs, then loosely braid or twist them together, working down until you get to the end of the strands. Use another piece of string to secure the strands together at the bottom of the "rope" you've now made. Next, overlap the two ends of the "rope" to form the circular shape of a wreath. If you'll be wearing the wreath, test the size at this stage to make sure it's a good fit before you make it permanent. If the wreath is a bit misshapen, just work it with your hands and bend it carefully into place until you're satisfied. Once you are happy with the size and shape of your wreath, use the excess string on each end to tie it all together into a circle. Add more string as necessary to securely bind everything in place, then tuck in or trim off any extra bits.

Next, attach the flowers. Simply tuck the stems through the openings in the braided wreath, and secure with string if needed. If you like, invite goddess energies of femininity, beauty, and compassion to enter the wreath. Your Beltane flower wreath is now ready to hang on the door or wear on your head as a material representation of springtime energies.

## Beltane Maypole

Maypoles have their roots in the early Germanic Paganism practiced throughout parts of Europe during the Iron Age and medieval periods. Their symbolism has been linked to the World Tree and the world axis, but most commonly, the Maypole with its phallic shape is considered a symbol of fertility. While the Maypole tradition may have evolved from older practices of simply decorating the living trees at Beltane, at the time the tradition really took root in Europe, it was common for Maypoles to be made from a tree that had been cut down especially for the purpose. Men would head into the woods to seek the tallest tree for the Maypole well ahead of the actual celebration. Sometimes, the Yule tree was saved and recycled as the next year's Maypole.

The Maypoles were erected in public areas where the whole community could see them. The pole was originally decorated with garlands and wreaths of flowers and leaves, and later, colorful ribbons were added. Villagers, especially young maidens, would dance around the Maypole in hopes of bringing fertility and good fortune to the community.

*Full-size Maypole*

If you'd like to make your own Maypole this Beltane, go for it! It's not nearly as daunting as it might sound, and you won't even have to cut down any trees in the process. Here's how to do it.

*You will need:*
Long, straight tree branch or dowel rod: at least 6 or 7 feet long, preferably
Ribbons, flowers, leaves, or other decorations as desired
Shovel, and/or 5 gallon flower pot or other container and enough rocks or dirt to fill it
Thumbtacks (optional)
Paint (optional)

Maypoles can be as tall as twenty-five feet or more, but that type of stature is a bit unfeasible for most modern Pagans living in urban areas. Fortunately, your Maypole doesn't need to be nearly that large. As long as the Maypole is taller than you are, it will be sufficient for Maypole dancing, and if you're not planning to dance but rather just use the Maypole for a decoration, it can be smaller still. You could make a cute little three-foot-tall Maypole, or a nice and sturdy ten-foot-tall Maypole—let your own preferences and possibly the nosiness of your neighbors dictate! Just keep in mind that the taller and heavier the pole, the more difficult it will be to keep it safely upright. If it's your first time making a Maypole and you don't have much help, I would definitely lean toward a shorter, lightweight pole.

Instead of cutting down a living tree, try to find a branch that has already fallen. You'll want one that's as straight as possible. Choosing a branch that's around seven feet tall and about an inch and a half in diameter is a good zone to shoot for. Remove any extra twigs, and you're good to go. If you can't find such a branch, you can use dowel rods or even a shower curtain rod to serve as the pole. Not quite as natural, but hey, a witch has to make do sometimes!

You'll probably want to at least partially decorate your Maypole before you erect it, especially if it's very tall. If you're using ribbons, cut the ribbons so that they're about twice as long as the Maypole itself. Tie these around the top of the pole so that they'll trail down on all sides. If you like, you can use thumbtacks to further secure the ribbons in place. If you don't want to use thumbtacks, just take another length of ribbon and wrap it around the pole right underneath the ribbons. Wrap the ribbon around the pole several times and tie it with large, bulky knots so that it creates a thicker base that will prevent the upper ribbons from sliding down.

Next, use ribbon to attach any flowers, leaves, garlands, or other ornamentation to the pole's upper portion. You might want to spiral a length of ribbon all the way down the pole from top to bottom to give the barber's pole or candy cane effect. If you like, use paint to add symbols that are personal to you or that you feel are especially fitting for the holiday. There's no "right way" to decorate a Maypole. Let your personal creativity and sense of aesthetics guide you. You can go ahead and completely decorate your Maypole now, or save some of the fun for when your Maypole has been set upright.

How you erect and secure your Maypole will depend on its height and weight. Obviously, the heavier and taller it is, the tougher your job will be. With a medium to large-sized pole, you'll need to dig a hole about twelve inches deep, submerge the bottom end of the Maypole, and fill the hole back in with dirt, taking care to firmly pack the soil around the base of the pole. Take care that it doesn't wobble. If your Maypole is over ten feet in height or over two inches in diameter, you will most likely need to secure it with other means, such as poured concrete or a sturdy wooden base, both beyond the scope of this simple arts and crafts tutorial. If you have a smaller, decorative Maypole that's six feet tall or shorter and not too heavy, you'll probably be able to skip the hole digging. Just fill a five-gallon flowerpot or other large container with a mixture of dirt and rocks, then bury the end of the Maypole in it. Place a thick layer of rock on top to keep the pole from shifting.

Once your Maypole is vertical, add any finishing touches to the decorations. Dedicate the Maypole with a dance, inviting friends to join you, if possible. Maypole dancing can get extremely complex, but it's actually not hard to do a simplified version. Make a circle around the pole, and have every other person stand a little closer in toward the center. Those people standing closer in toward the pole spin and twirl in the opposite direction from the people standing farther back. Each holding the end of a length of ribbon, the dancers in the "inner loop" cross under the ribbon next to them, moving to the outer rim of the circle as the neighboring dancer moves forward to the center. If that's still a little complicated, try a simple, free-flowing dance, just letting your heart guide your body and allowing your soul to enjoy the moment. If you don't have anyone to dance with, notice the birds, insects, and animals around you as you celebrate around the Maypole.

## Beltane Decor

Beltane is essentially a celebration of love, light, and the joy of warmer weather, and decorating for the holiday should be every bit as easy and breezy. By following a few simple guidelines and adding some special touches here and there, your home will be ready for Beltane in no time. Let's first cover the basics, then we'll go over some specific ideas for festive decor you can make on a budget.

## Let In the Light!

The most essential "rule" of Beltane decorating is to keep it light and airy. Open the curtains, pull up the shades, throw open the windows! Let the sun shine in. It's hard to get into the Beltane spirit if your home is dark and dismal. If you're lacking in the window department, consider buying extra floor lamps to help illuminate your home. At night, burn candles for a natural touch that will help you attune with the element of fire, considered an especially prominent force at Beltane.

To make the most of your home's lighting, keep fabrics and colors light, as well. Choose lightweight cottons and linens or gauzy fabrics over heavier materials, and use darker colors like deep browns, dark grays, navy blues, and black only sparingly.

## Bring In the Green!

Another primary theme of Beltane decorating is to highlight the beauty of nature wherever possible, and what better way to do that than to bring some of that nature into the home? Use fresh flowers generously, placing bouquets of wild flowers in unlikely places around your house, or hanging floral garlands from banisters and mantles. Yellow flowers are especially well suited, being the color most often associated with the sun. Ferns and other green houseplants are good additions, too, supplying a palpable energy of vitality and growth. If you have pets or small children, however, just make sure that any flowers or other plants you use are nontoxic.

### Make It Romantic!

Love is in the air at Beltane, so let it be in your home's decor as well. Keep everything neat and clean and uncluttered, and add romantic touches where possible. Soft fabrics, extra pillows, a bit of lace here or there, a smattering of fresh rose petals, a couple of old photographs, a picture of the sea or the sunrise … a small addition here or there can go a long way in reminding your guests of life's finer things. Just don't overdo it—no one wants to feel like they've walked right into an ultra cheesy Valentine's Day card! Use potpourri and essential oils to give your home a lovely fragrance and a romantic feel—jasmine and rose are both highly effective in promoting feelings of closeness and passion.

### DIY Beltane Decor

Now that we've covered the basics, let's get down to discussing some cool ways you can make your home look extra festive for the holiday using just a few special touches requiring very little, if any, money.

*Mini Tabletop Maypole*

## Mini Maypole Centerpiece

This easy-to-make decoration will add a festive touch to a dining table or side table. All you'll need is a dish, some potpourri, a stick, some ribbon, and a small hunk of modeling clay. To get started, find a smooth stick about seven to eight inches long. Wrap the stick with ribbon, spiraling it around from top to bottom down the length of the stick and tying it at both ends to keep it in place. Next, tie several ribbons to the top of the stick so that you'll have a piece of ribbon trailing down each side. Put the base of the stick into a small hunk of modeling clay, then place this in the middle of the dish. Fill the dish with potpourri, arrange the ribbons around the sides, and your Beltane centerpiece is complete.

## Fire and Water Altar

Beltane marks the time of symbolic union between the Goddess and the God, a time when opposites attract and polarities fall in sync. A fire and water altar is a perfect way to honor nature's tides while giving your home a heavy dose of magickal pizzazz.

You can use any small platform for your altar. A coffee table, end table, or even a cardboard box weighted down with books or the like will do. Cover the altar in a cloth colored in tune with the holiday: green or brown would work nicely, as they're associated equally with both the Goddess and the God, but yellow, white, pink, silver, or gold would be appropriate, as well.

For the centerpiece of the altar, fill a large, clear bowl with water, inviting the Goddess energies and the element of water to enter into it. Place floating candles in the water and light them, invoking the God and the element of fire as you do so.

Decorate the rest of the altar with objects in silver and gold, representing the Goddess and the God, the moon and the sun, water and fire, respectively. Add flowers and other fresh vegetation for a boost of color, and your altar is ready for Beltane magick.

### Ribbons on the Ceiling, Flowers in the Sky

If you're having a Beltane party, consider this design for your main party room or dancing area. All you'll need is some colorful ribbon, thumbtacks, paperclips, or tape, and a large handful of fresh or artificial flowers. Cut the ribbon in lengths long enough to stretch from the center of the room to each corner, allowing for some slack so that the ribbon can drape down rather than be held taut. Attach the ribbons to the center of the ceiling with a thumbtack. Use more thumbtacks to attach the loose ends of the ribbons to points in the corners and the middle of the walls of the room, using at least six strands of ribbon. Hang them like party streamers, so that they drape down, but not so far down that your guests will hit their heads on them.

Next, add flowers, either real or artificial. The artificial ones won't look quite as cool, but they'll look nice for a lot longer than perishable fresh flowers. Use paperclips or tape to attach the real or faux blossoms at random points along the length of the ribbons. Place a big bouquet right at the center point where the ribbons meet, and your Beltane party hall is complete.

## Don't Forget the Yard!

If you want your home to look super festive this Beltane, don't keep all your awesome decorations indoors. Spice up the outside of your home, too, using ribbons, flowers, and additional greenery. Hang a floral wreath on your door, attach some greenery to your mailbox, hang ribbons and flowers from trees and shrubs. You might even make a traditional May Bush, decorating a small tree or bush with ribbons, flowers, garlands, and painted seashell ornaments. Don't forget to remove dead branches or other yard waste that might be cluttering up your yard so that Nature's living beauty is allowed to shine.

PRAYERS
AND
INVOCATIONS

...tance, growth, passion, love, union, cooperation, fertility fairy

...tection, purification, manifestation, handfastings; building sacred

...visiting sacred wells; giving offerings, working with faeries, vita...

...alking the boundaries of one's property, protecting plants, divin...

...nimals, people, and possessions astronomical midpoint, and sun...

...the spring equinox and summer solstice. Sun at 15 degrees of...

...n the northern hemisphere, Sun at 15 degrees of Scorpio in...

...uthern hemisphere. Female: Maiden Goddess, Mother Godd...

...Earth Goddess, water plants or animals, the Lover preparin...

...with her beloved Flora, Danu, Freyja, Maia, Shasti, Pros...

...Chin-hua fu-jen, Venus, Diana, Artemis, Aphrodite, Astar...

...ona, Rauni, Sarasvati, Horae, Pan, Cernunnos, Beal, Bal...

...Pluto Wotan, Odin, Oak King, Apollo, Ra, Mugwort...

...ertility, protection, divination, communication, with spirits ener...

...purification, joy, love, prophetic dreams, renewal energy, vitality...

...wealth, fairy magick, luck success, strength Rose, Frankincens...

...asmine, Lemon, Pine, Mint visiting sacred wells; giving off...

...dance abundance, growth, passion, love, union, cooperation, fert...

...tection, purification, manifestation, handfastings; building sacred

*W*HILE SOME PRAYER takes the form of a humble plea for assistance made to an almighty, parental god, for many Pagans, prayer is more of a hands-on experience, a blending of spellwork and communication with spirits involving active emotional, mental, and spiritual concentration and a delicate application of flattery, intention, faith, rhythm, repetition, visualization, and other magickal techniques.

When we talk about Pagan prayer, it should be noted that Pagan spirituality doesn't necessarily demand an anthropomorphic understanding of the deities. Gods can be viewed as anthropomorphic beings, certainly, but they might alternatively be viewed as thoughtforms, spirits, symbols, allegories, egregores, or simply enormous collections of energy, each with its own unique attributes, power, purpose, and potential. Just as a pentagram is a symbol encompassing the energy of the five elements, so too might a god be understood in one sense as a type of übersymbol, encompassing the energy of anything and everything that godform represents.

We all have our own unique understandings of deity, and it's imperative that we go about prayer with full authenticity and genuineness based on these understandings. Whatever our personal concept of deity might be, a prayer is a direct attempt to elicit any help or assistance that deity can offer. To many Neopagans, the buck doesn't stop with the gods—there is often a strong belief also in personal responsibility for one's choices and the consequences those choices lead to. We're humble enough to ask for help, but not so helpless that we don't realize that a large part of our fate is indeed in our own living, magickal hands. When we pray to the gods, we might feel that we are also praying to ourselves, praying to the world, or praying to activate that magickal spark that can only be fueled by the light of hope. We are the gods and the gods are we; when we pray, we are asking ourselves to remember that while at the same time acknowledging that we are not all that is.

An invocation is different from a prayer. Invocation is the process of actually calling into a person or thing the energetic spirit of a particular godform or other entity. The person or object becomes the godform, an open channel through which the summoned spirit can come in and make itself manifest in the mundane physical world. When invoking a spirit into yourself, first empty your mind of thoughts related to your own personal life or identity. Let go of ego, and try as best you can to open up, becoming an empty vessel into which the spirit can pour.

This chapter contains a collection of prayers and invocations created especially for Beltane. Incorporate them into rituals and spellwork, use them as guides for meditation or journaling, or simply use them on their own as a way to get closer to the divine energies of the season. Crafted with tried-and-true principles of spoken and written magick in mind, these prayers and invocations are designed for maximum effectiveness. However, do feel free to adapt, expand, edit, and elaborate as you wish.

## Green Man Invocation

Green Man, I invoke thee!

King of the woods, lord of the wild, master of beasts,
  come into me!

I am the earth. I am the field. I am the vessel,
  come into me!

Fill me with your lust! Your life! Your power!

Great Green Man, I invoke thee!

By your names I summon thee.

Cernunnos, Pan, king of the woods, lord of the wild, master
  of beasts, come into me!

You are the Horned God. You are the Oak King. You are the
  god who dies and is resurrected.

Pan! Cernunnos! Green Man! Come into me!

I empty myself for you, lord.

I ready myself for you, lord.

Ride me, Green Man, ride me,

and we'll fly through the night,

through the forests,

through the trees,

beside the stream of life everlasting.

Touch through my hands, taste through my tongue, see
through my eyes, feel through my body!

Run with my legs, reach with my arms, breathe with my
lungs, love with my heart!

It is not I but the Green Man who speaks with this voice!

Ride me, Green Man, ride me!

## *Prayer to the Green Man*

Great Green Man, dear Lord of the Forests,

king of the woods, master of the fields and fowl, god of the
rocks and the trees!

Great Green Man, I pray to you! Please hear me now!

Fill me with life and energy! Protect my health!

My body is your body, Green Man, and it thrives and grows
like the leaves of the grass and the trees.

Great Green Man, I pray to you!

I am a sapling and you are the grove.

Great Green Man, I pray to you, make me your own!

Fill my pockets with riches! Protect my wealth and bring me
prosperity!

My treasure is your treasure, Green Man, and it shines like the
    sun on the grass and the trees!
Great Green Man, I pray to you!
I am the acorn and you are the oak.
Great Green Man, I pray to you, make me your own!
Make me strong like the forest, alive like the trees, busy like
    the bees!
Make me bold and alive, my lord!
Make me strong; help me thrive, my lord!
Great Green Man, I pray to you, make me your own!
A child of the forest, a babe of the trees, your servant, your
    steward, your friend, and your liege.
I am the budding branch. I am the tender shoot. I am the
    climbing vine. I am the thirsty root.
Look after me, Green Man, and make me your own!
Great Green Man, I pray to you, make me your own!

## Solar Invocation

Bel, Belenos, Belemos, Beal!
Bright one, shining one,
everlasting light one!
The sun is your eye, its rays are your tears,
with life comes destruction, with new days die the years.
Great Belenos endures, the bright one shines on,
the everlasting light one shining brightly ever on!

Belenos, turn me on!

I am the torch, the lamp, the wick!

Fill me with your light, Belenos!

Belenos, turn me on!

Enter into my body.

Fill me with brightness.

Fill me with light.

Fill me with fire.

Belenos, turn me on and enter into me!

I am the leaf absorbing sunlight. I am the branch engulfed in
flame.

I am yours, Great Belenos, light me up and turn me on!

## Prayer to Belenos

Dear Belenos, Bright One, Shining One, Great One!

You whose light is unending;

you whose warmth never ceases;

you whose effort never wanes!

Dear Belenos, Great Belenos, I pray to you.

Shine upon me, bright one!

Fuel my dreams, shining one!

Bless me with your light.

Bless me with your love.

Bless me with your energy, your strength, your passion!

Transform me with your fire.

Make me worthy of your light.

Let me shine with infinite brightness and love as you do,

Lord Belenos!

Great Belenos, please bless me.

Shine upon my dreams, my fields, my flocks!

Shine upon the earth and all its beasts!

Chase away the darkness, Great Belenos.

Chase away the fears and doubts and cold.

Chase away the darkness, Great Belenos.

Chase away the darkness with your never-ending light!

## Earth Goddess Invocation

Lovely maiden, beautiful goddess of the earth, the fields,
the flowers, the trees.

Lady of the oceans, ruler of the rivers and seas,

great mother of the beasts and the birds, I invoke you!

Great Lady of the wild wood, Great Lover of the world,

Great Danu, maiden of stars and mother of earth,

I invoke you!

You are the Lover and the Beloved. You are the sun and the
moon. You are the death and the life.

Great goddess, great Danu, lovely maiden, I invoke you!

Come into me, Goddess, and meet your consort.

My body is your body, my pleasure is your pleasure, my lust
is your lust.

Come into me, Goddess, and find your lover who awaits!

Come into me, Danu, and accept the sun king's seed.

Come into me, Danu, and make me blossom like the flowers
and trees.

Great goddess, great Danu, lovely maiden, mother of the
earth, I invoke you!

Great Danu, I invoke you! I am yours, and you are me.

## Prayer to the Earth Goddess

Great Goddess, my mother, my lover,

I pray to you.

Let me open myself to the blessings that come.

Let me give myself over to ecstasy!

Let me open myself to love!

As the soil accepts the seed, as the leaves absorb the sun,
as the earth soaks up the rain,

let me be as you, the empty page, the foundation for the
living word.

I am the gateway. I am the womb of creation.

I am the mother, the maiden, the crone, the earth, the moon,
the stars, and the sun.

I am you, Great Goddess, and you are everything.

I am open to blessings.

I am open to ecstasy.

I am open to love.

I am the beautiful lover awaiting the beloved.
As I love you, Great Goddess, so too will my beloved come!
Great Goddess, you are the key to the creation.
You are the soil and the rain, the oceans and the darkness,
    the moon and the stars and the sun.
Nothing would be without you, Great Goddess, as you
    encompass all that can be.
You are the lover and the loved, the bride and the groom,
    the maiden earth and her beloved, the sun!
Great Goddess, let us blossom and bloom with a beauty
    that is fit for our king!
Bring me love!
Bring me ecstasy!
Bring me blessings!
I and the Goddess will it, and so it is bound to be!

## Invocation of Flora

Lovely Flora, pretty lady, you whose beauty is brighter than
    the stars,
shinier than the seas, more glorious than the moon itself!
Lovely Flora, pretty lady, grace me, embrace me, enter into
    me, amaze me!
May your spirit come into my heart!
May your love flow through me!
May your beauty and bliss embrace me!

You are the queen of the flowers.

You are the beautiful blossoming earth.

You are the sprout that pushes through the flat field to reach the sun!

All the flowers of the earth reflect your love.

All the beauty of the earth is but your song.

You are the rose that opens and closes.

You are the love that is only its own.

Lovely Flora, pretty lady, come into my heart!

I am a flower awaiting your presence, a blossom that's ready to bloom!

Come into my heart, lovely Flora, enter into me, grace me, amaze me!

Embrace me and cause me to bloom!

## Prayer to Flora

Lady Flora, beautiful one, you who are loved by all!

Lady Flora, I ask you to bring me love.

Let me be a mirror of your beauty and your charm.

Let me attract and entice the persons I desire, just as the bees are drawn to the blossom's sweet scent!

Lady Flora, Lovely Flora, I ask you, I beg you, I leave you no course but to bring me love!

If my lover doesn't find me, may the roses wilt and wither!

May the lilies dry up forevermore!

Lady Flora, bring me love and the gardens will blossom
    evermore!
Lady Flora, I give you my love! I give you my heart!
I give you my oath and my word!
Bring me my love, Lady Flora, lead them through you,
    and unto me!
Like a bee to a flower, my lover is drawn to me!
Lady Flora, we will it, and so it will be!

## Solar Invocation for Growth

Use this solar invocation to summon into an object or a plant an
energy conducive to growth. For example, you might use the
invocation to draw the powers of the sun into a paintbrush you
plan to use to paint a masterpiece, thus ensuring an enormous
supply of creative energy as you craft your artwork. As another
possibility, you might use the invocation to empower your garden plants with an extra boost of solar energy that's bound to
help them grow.

Great sun, Sol, Ra, Bright One, Shining One!
You are the great eye, you are the fire, you are the light!
Great sun, I hold you in my hand.
I place you where I like.
And you are here, great sun, great Ra, great Shining One,
    great Bright One!

You are here now in the place that I place you,
you are here now and shining so bright.
Great sun, Sol, Ra, Bright One, Shining One!
You are the hope! You are the fire! You are the light!
Great sun, great Sol, I implore you!
Shine here where I place you, day or night.

## Invocation of Belenos into the Fire

Use this invocation to call the spirit of Belenos into the Beltane fire. If you can't build a bonfire or a smaller campfire, you can still use this invocation to summon Belenos into a candle flame. The size of the fire doesn't matter, as the portal to the realm of spirit is created like a pinprick in a balloon: once the illusion of separation between the worlds is penetrated in any way, it's a bust. Belenos can slip into a tiny candle flame just as easily as pouring forth from a large torrent of fire. Utilize this invocation to summon Belenos into the Beltane fire, then communicate with that spirit in whatever ways you see fit, perhaps saying thanks, or perhaps asking for courage, energy, strength, or other qualities you admire. You can also ask Belenos for answers. Think of a yes or no question, then observe the behavior of the Beltane fire. If the flames lean toward you, it signifies an answer of yes, and if the flames shy away from you, the answer is a likely no.

Belenos, Beal, Bel, Shining One, you who are fire!
You who are heat! You who are light! You who are bright!
Come into this flame, enter into this fire!
To you this fire is dedicated, Great Belenos; to you this fire
    now becomes your home.
Enter into the flame! Enter into the fire!
Great Belenos, you must enter into it now! Enter into the
    flame! Enter into the fire!
Shine upon us, Belenos! Warm us, Belenos! Make us strong,
    great Belenos!
Great Belenos, come witness through your light!
Be with us now, great Belenos!
The flames are your body; our desires, the wood!
Be with us, Belenos, and burn up the wood!
Be in the fire, and burn up the wood!
Enter into the fire; enter into the flames!
Enter into us, Belenos, we call you by name!
Beal is the fire, and this fire is Beal's!
This fire is Beal. This fire is Beal!
Be with us, Belenos, come into the flame!
Come into the fire!
We all know your name!

# Prayer for the Protection of Plants and Animals

Lord and Lady of the wild wood, Lord and Lady of the May!
King of the forests and Queen of the fields! Listen to me,
　　a creature, an animal of the earth!
Your children are in trouble! The foxes, the hounds,
　　and the wolves!
The horses and cows! The bears and the squirrels!
　　The birds and the fish!
The humans and all the other living beasts!
Great Mother, Great Father, we need you now!
Protect your children! We need you now!
Shield the animals from unnatural dangers.
　　Protect us all from cruelty.
Give us habitat, food, shelter, water. Let us breed and grow
　　and thrive.
Guide our hands, guide our minds, guide our hearts so we
　　can stay alive!
Protect us, Lord and Lady! Protect your living beasts!
Lord and Lady of the wild wood! Lord and Lady of the May!
King of the forests and Queen of the fields! Listen to me,
　　a human, a steward of the earth!
Your garden is in trouble! The trees, the herbs, the blooms!
The flowers and the grasses! The roots and the leaves!
The vines and the gourds!
The fruit and all the seeds!

Great Mother, Great Father, we need you now!
Protect your children! We need you now!
Shield the plants from unnatural dangers. Protect the trees
and herbs from man.
Give the plants sun and rain and soil and protection.
Let the plants live and grow and thrive.
Guide our hands, guide our minds, guide our hearts so the
earth can stay alive!
Lord and Lady of the wild wood, Lord and Lady of the May!
I ask you with my heart and mind, protect the beasts and
plants in kind!

## Prayer to the Faeries

According to early Celtic belief, faeries are out and about most
prevalently at the times of Samhain and Beltane. While the
faeries of Celtic lore were fearsome creatures to be avoided
or appeased rather than befriended, many Neopagans think of
faeries as generally benevolent and often helpful nature spirits, believed to be just as fond of making merry as they are of
making mischief. If there's a lot of stagnation in your life, or
you feel you could use a boost of extra luck in a particular situ-
ation, you might consider giving some faery magick a try this
Beltane. Here's a prayer you can use to ask the faeries to please
help you out.

Sweet faeries, blessed Fae, queens of magick and the night!
Wonderful faeries, powerful faeries, blessed mistresses of
moonlight and of fate!
Be my allies on this night, and come help me with my plight!
Sweet faeries, blessed Fae, queens of magick and the night!
I invite you faeries to spread your mischief! Work your
magick! Change my fate!
I ask you faeries to make it happen! My wish come true
before it's too late!
Sweet faeries! Blessed faeries! Powerful allies in the night!
By your whims, the fences broken; by your wish,
the gates unlocked.
By your will, the mirror shatters; by your voice,
the serpent stops.
Be my allies, little faeries, be my allies in my plight!
Be my allies as I wish it, change my fate this very night!

RITUALS
OF
CELEBRATION

dance, growth, passion love, union, cooperation, fertility faery
tection, purification, manifestation, handfastings, building sacred
visiting sacred wells, giving offerings, working with faeries, ritual
lking the boundaries of one's property, protecting plants, divine
nimals, people, and possessions astronomical midpoint, and sum
the spring equinox and summer solstice: Sun at 15 degrees of
n the northern hemisphere, Sun at 15 degrees of Scorpio in t
uthern hemisphere. Female: Maiden Goddess, Mother Godde
Earth Goddess, water plants or animals, the Lover preparing
with her beloved Flora, Danu, Freyja, Maia, Shasti, Pros
Chin-hua fu-jen, Venus, Diana, Artemis, Aphrodite, Astart
ona, Rauni, Sarasvati, Horae, Pan, Cernunnos, Beal, Bald
Pluto Wotan, Odin, Oak King, Apollo, Ra, Mugwort Lu
ertility, protection, divination, communication, with spirits energy
purification, joy, love, prophetic dreams, renewal energy, vitality
wealth, fairy magick, luck success, strength Rose, Frankincense
asmine, Lemon, Pine, Mint visiting sacred wells, giving offer
terus, abundance, growth, passion, love, union, cooperation, ferti
tection, purification, manifestation, handfastings, building sacred

$\mathcal{B}$ELTANE IS A time of fertility, a time of union, a time of manifestation, a time of love. It's a great time for rituals filled with fun, gratitude, creativity, and passion. In this chapter, you'll find several rituals especially crafted to help you connect with these powerful energies and make the most of their marvelous magickal potential.

Rituals differ from spells in that they're typically, but not always, more complex, more in-depth, lengthier to perform, and result in longer-lasting effects. Rituals usually involve direct communication and contact with higher spiritual entities, be they elemental forces, deities, or various godforms, whereas a spell may or may not incorporate such powers. While a ritual might certainly include elements of magick and spellwork (the ones below do), there is also a spiritual purpose, a value found solely in the *experience* of the ritual, completely independent from outcome. In contrast, spells *always* have a magickal purpose, and may or may not include a spiritual purpose.

Below you'll find a ritual designed for solitary practice, a ritual to do with a partner, a ritual to do with a larger group, and a super quick mini-ritual to do when you only have a few moments to spare. All the rituals described can be safely adapted, so feel free to add to them and adjust so that your ritual experience reflects your own uniqueness as a magickal and spiritual being.

## Beltane Growth Ritual for Solitary Practice

This ritual is intended to honor growth, both the growing things of the earth and the ever-evolving soul within the individual magickal practitioner. Though especially designed for solitary use, the ritual format here described can easily be adapted to group practice. If you have friends joining you for the rite, just do everything in unison, or take turns handling different parts of the ritual according to aptitudes and interests. Do feel free to adapt and enhance these basic ritual proceedings to better suit your own personal beliefs and preferences.

### *Purpose:*

Attune with nature's tides, attain deeper understanding of the process of growth as it occurs within nature and within one's self, express gratitude for the growth of vegetation that sustains us, contemplate and "take stock" of personal growth, initiate and manifest opportunities for even greater personal growth.

## Setting:

Outside, in the morning

## Supplies:

Two tea light candles or taper candles with candleholders:
    preferably one gold or yellow, one silver or white
Fresh plants, herbs, and flowers from your region,
    roots attached
Large bowl of water
Two pieces of paper and a pen
One small square of green fabric and a piece of gold or
    yellow string

## Pre-Ritual Preparations:

Take a bath or a shower to help cleanse away both physical
and psychic impurities. Imagine any negativity or staleness
flowing out of you and into the water as it washes over you. If
you like, add a handful of sea salt to the bath water to help you
attune with solar energies. If you're having a shower, try rub-
bing your skin with sugar or oatmeal to shed away unwanted
vibrations while connecting to Beltane themes of sweetness
and abundance.

Go skyclad, with no clothes whatsoever, or dress in something you feel is suitable for a growth ritual. Natural fabrics in
shades of green would be an excellent choice. You'll want something comfortable that helps you feel natural, strong, and earthy.

For an added boost of magickal power, accessorize with gold or copper jewelry, both attuned with solar energies.

Make a list of accomplishments, noting all the ways you've grown as a person over the past year. Make another list outlining any new goals for personal growth that you would like to achieve this season.

Place the bowl of water on top of the list of past accomplishments. Arrange the candles on either side of the bowl, placing the gold or yellow candle to the right, and the white or silver candle to the left. Place the fresh plants in front of the bowl, on top of the list of new goals for personal growth.

### The Ritual:

Sit and place your palms flat down on the ground. Take several deep breaths until you feel calm and centered. Then extend this feeling of calm outward beyond the boundaries of your physical body, so that it encompasses and encloses the entire ritual space. Stand up and walk a clockwise circle around the space, while at the same time projecting a light, loving energy through your chest, flat palms, eyes, or wand tip. If you're having trouble feeling it, it might help to think of something or someone you love very deeply, then let that emotion radiate outward, illuminating the ritual area in a bright, white light. Another idea is to walk around the space while ringing a bell, which acts as a quick and fairly foolproof method of clearing away stale, negative energies while at the same time inviting fresh, positive energy. The area surrounding you is now filled with a peaceful vibration, you're ready to delve into the heart of the ritual.

Look around you. Notice the plants, their growth dependent on the interplay of the earth, sun, and rain. Touch the ground, stroking the living plants that spring from the earth beneath you. Do you feel the powerful energy of the earth, vibrating with life and creation, throbbing like a heartbeat, pulsating with both love and indifference?

Let this energy come into you, literally pulling it into your body through the point of contact between your hands and the living earth. This might sound like an oversimplification, but it isn't. You have the ability to move and direct energy through the conscious application of your will and intention.

Think about what you want to happen energy-wise, then let your feelings guide you, noticing how your body responds throughout the process. If you're actually moving or directing energy into or through your body, there's usually a physical sensation that goes along with it. You might feel the energy moving through your body as a subtle tingle, as a strong and sudden jolt, "shock," or shiver, as a feeling of heaviness or lightness, or as a sensation of warmth or coolness.

Sensations vary depending on the individual, but certain energies do seem to have outstanding characteristics a great many of us experience very similarly. In this ritual, for instance, the earth energy you're invoking into your body is likely to have a warm, strong, vibrant feel. As you start to feel it, let it take over, allowing it reign over your body and emotion until any sense of ego is nil. If you like, rub some dirt on your skin or touch your body with green plants or flowers to enhance the feeling. You've now invoked the earth element, the powers of which are now filling you completely and flowing through you freely.

Next, turn your attentions to the bowl of water. Think of the rivers, the oceans, the lakes, the seas, and think of the rain that fills them. Think of the water beneath the earth, above the earth, and on the earth. Drink from the bowl, envisioning the water as the flow of a river or droplets of cool rain. Notice how your body feels as the water moves through you, quenching thirst and fueling transformation. Invite this energy to stay within you for the course of the ritual. Having now invoked both earth and water, envision yourself as the damp soil, wet and dark and warm as a womb.

Pick up the fresh plants that you've placed on top of the list of new goals you'd like to achieve. Read over the list as you cradle the plants gently in your open hands. Think of these plants as the very hopes and dreams outlined on the list of goals, and feel the emotion within those desires. Let that energy pour into the plants, charging them with a feeling of love and filling them also with the powers of earth and water that should still be coursing freely throughout your body. Place the plants in the water and say:

*These are the dreams of* (insert your own full name),
*a child of the earth, moon, sun, and sea.*

Light the silver or white candle, representative of the moon. Hold the candle above the bowl and think of the gravitational pull of the moon literally moving the oceans, manifesting and directing the tides of the water that covers more than 70 percent of our planet's surface. Think of how the tides affect the weather, and how the weather in turn affects the lives of Earth's plants and animals. Think also of the fact that your body's composition is more than 50 percent water, and how, like the seas, the moon sways our inner emotional tides, as well. Let the idea of your dependence on the moon sink in, then allow your feelings of gratitude to flow into the candle flame and into the water below. Think of your list of past accomplishments that lies beneath the bowl of water, and think of the new dreams you want to achieve, represented by the plants you've placed in the bowl. With your hand that's not holding the candle, swirl the water in the bowl clockwise as you say:

*Great moon, as you move the sea, so too move me!*

Watch the plants swirl around in the water and envision your goals manifesting, tides turning in your favor thanks to the help of the moon.

Return the candle to its place at the left side of the bowl.

Next, light the gold or yellow candle, representative of the sun. Hold the candle up to the sun, and think about the sunlight streaming into the candle flame, adding solar energy to its already bright and fiery power. Walk clockwise around the ritual space, noticing how the living plants that spring from the ground seem to pulsate with the same solar charge now infused within the candle flame. Invite that solar charge to flow into you, also. Let the candle flame draw the sunlight, then direct the energy down through the wax and into your body. As you walk around the circle, envision the plants around you growing, fueled by the sunlight, earth, and water. Stop in front of the bowl of water and hold the candle high above it.

Envision yourself growing and sense the cellular and molecular processes going on within your body, just as dependent on the sunlight, earth, and water as the vegetation surrounding you. Think about the process of photosynthesis that occurs within the green parts of plants, a process in which pure sunlight is transformed into nutrients that fuel the plant's growth. Look now at the plants floating in the bowl of water before you. Feel the solar energy still pulsating within your body, warm and bright, fiery and strong. Ask the sun itself to help you fuel your dreams, then direct all that amplified solar power now coursing through you and through the candle to enter into the plants in the bowl. As you do so, envision yourself growing ten feet tall, a thriving giant radiating with health, vigor, and success, just like a mighty tree playing king of the forest. Say:

> *Great sun, fuel and energy of Earth,*
> *charge me up now, give my future dreams birth!*

Place the candle back in its spot to the right of the basin. Let both candles burn out completely, and leave the basin of water with the plants in it outside overnight. Place the list of new goals in a sunny spot in your home. The list of past accomplishments you can keep for sentimental purposes or discard; its magickal work is done. The next morning, remove the plants from the bowl and set them in the sun to dry. Pour the water on the earth. Once the plants are dried, tie them up in the small piece of cloth (preferably green for growth), and secure the bundle with the length of gold or yellow thread, colored in tune with powerful solar vibrations. Place the bundle on top of the list of new goals that should be sitting somewhere in your home in a sunny spot. The rite now complete, you should feel very much in tune with Beltane's energy flow, and your inner process of personal and spiritual growth will be highly accelerated, at least temporarily. Make the most of it!

# *Beltane Handfasting Ritual for Lasting Union*

This Beltane handfasting ritual is designed to create a lasting union and forge a cooperative, happy, and loving marital partnership between two people. With the concept of sacred union as its framework, this handfasting ritual is moving and powerful, offering a meaningful Pagan alternative to more mainstream marriage ceremonies.

## *Purpose:*

This ritual is designed to unite two people into the bonds of marriage. A handfasting ritual is a type of binding magick, tying together the spiritual energies of the two individuals so that a new union is created and the boundaries and limitations of that union are established and fortified.

## *Setting:*

Evening, preferably outdoors

## *Supplies:*

One red candle, to symbolize both love and the element
of fire
One glass of water with ice, preferably in a clear, blue,
or silver cup

## Pre-Ritual Preparations:

You'll need to decide which role each participant will play in the rite. This ritual has two starring roles: the part of fire, and the part of water. Let personal preferences guide your selection, or consider having the person with the more masculine, dominant, or active personality play the role of fire while the person with the more feminine, or softer, gentler personality, plays the role of water.

Going skyclad or donning special ritual attire can enrich the experience and enhance the magick. The person playing the part of fire might wear robes in red or orange to symbolize flame, gold or yellow in honor of the sun, or solid white to represent pure light. The person acting the role of water might wear translucent fabrics or clothing in shades of blue to symbolize water, or they might choose silver clothing to pay homage to the moon. Solid black attire is another fitting option, representing the darkness of deep water, the darkness beneath the ground where seeds begin to grow, and the darkness of the cosmic womb from which we all emerge.

If you're able to find a peaceful natural setting in which to do the ritual, the space will need very little preparation. Make sure the area is free of debris, and be sure it's a space where you'll feel safe and comfortable. If you're enacting the ritual indoors, choose a place that's clean and uncluttered. If the area you've chosen has a negative or stale feeling to it, you can do a general space clearing before you begin the ritual. One easy method of clearing an area of undesirable or stagnant energy is to sweep the space with a broom. Begin in the center of the ritual area and sweep toward the edges, moving in an outward, counterclockwise spiral while visualizing any stale or negative energies dissipating and dispersing. You might also perform a basic circle casting if you like, or simply light some incense and a few extra candles to enhance the magickal ambiance of the ritual space. If you like, enhance the space with fresh flowers.

### The Ritual:

Begin by facing one another, the person acting as fire holding the candle and the person acting as water holding the glass. Fire lights the candle, envisioning sunlight and flame radiating from their body's core as they do so, dissolving all traces of ego. Fire says:

*I am Fire. I am Sun. I am the warmth, the light, the seed,*
*and the will. I am* (insert your full name).

Water takes a sip from the glass, envisioning rivers, oceans, and rains flowing down their throat and integrating into their being as they swallow, letting the energetic vibration of the water overpower personality. Water says:

> *I am Water. I am Moon. I am the blood, the food, the womb,*
> *and the intention. I am* (insert your full name).

The person playing the role of water becomes the cosmic womb, while the person playing the role of fire becomes the fertilizing seed, a combination from which will spring the new creation—the new cooperative partnership between anima and animus. This is the sacred union, the magick of intermingling polarities that gives rise to creation and manifestation.

Imagine that you yourself are whatever it is you are representing—say it, open your heart and body to it, and invite those energies to flow through you. Be a vessel for whatever it is you are representing, and if you haven't already, try for a moment now to forget all about who you are in your everyday life. You are fire. You are water. You are the womb. You are the seed. You are the yin. You are the yang. Whatever it is, don't just think of it—*be* it to the greatest extent you can manage. It might sound tricky, but it's actually not that complicated. By emptying yourself of identity and ego (which *is* the tricky part!), you make yourself an open vessel for any energies you wish to temporarily "host" within your body. This is the process that is known as invocation, actually invoking, or taking within your own body, the spirit, entity, or energy you've invited for a visit.

Once both you and your ritual partner are fully "in the zone," in character with your respective roles and unhampered by mundane thoughts and feelings, look into each other's eyes and raise the energy. Think of the specific outcome you hope to achieve with the ritual, the main aim and purpose you're hoping to manifest. Feel the emotions of that reality, what it would be like and feel like to have a successful, lasting partnership. As you look into your partner's eyes, let the emotions you feel flow back and forth between you, magnifying with each "pass" until you sense the energy is at its highest vibration.

At this point, the person playing the part of Water opens himself or herself completely, envisioning a fertile field, a womb, and primordial darkness ready to embrace the spark of life. The person playing the role of fire should continue focusing on the ritual goal at hand (creating a permanent, loving bond), and when the vision and feeling of love and unity is clear in both mind and heart, every bit of energy they have within them is sent into the body and spirit of the person playing the role of water. Just envision the magickal power you've raised through emotion and visualization flowing out of your eyes and into the eyes of your partner. The person playing the part of water should feel this action if you do it right. It should feel like a powerful blast of emotionally charged energy.

Once the energy has been received by the person playing water, exchange the objects you are holding, passing the glass of water to fire and giving the candle to water. Both ritualists say:

*By our powers combined, by moon and by sun,*
*by water and fire, what we will, will be won!*

Fire takes a sip of water. Then, the cup and the candle are placed side by side on the altar. The partners clasp their hands together over the altar, gazing steadily into each other's eyes as they repeat in unison nine times:

*We are bound together, together forever!*

As this is said, the ritualists should envision ropes of golden light, made of pure love, circling around their wrists and entwining together their hands.

The partners share a loving, passionate kiss. Water then takes the ice cube out of the glass and holds it over the candle flame, melting the ice and putting out the candle.

Clasping hands once again, the partners say in unison:

*Our love remains through dark and light!*
*May love transform us, day and night!*

The partners share another kiss, and the handfasting ritual is complete.

# Beltane Group Ritual for Love

With fertile energies running wild, love is in the air this time of year, just waiting for us to reach out and grab it. Why not take advantage of the opportunity with a ritual centered on love and romance?

This Beltane group ritual is designed to help all participants attract, express, and manifest more love in their lives while tuning in to the fertile, creative energies of the day. It's most powerful when worked with larger groups of seven or more, but it can be performed by groups as small as four in number.

### Purpose:

This ritual will help participants improve their ability to attract, express, and manifest love. It will also help ritualists get into the romantic, carefree spirit of Beltane, and it can be useful in heightening creative energy and bringing fresh inspiration.

### Setting:

Nighttime, preferably outdoors, preferably in a wooded area or somewhere near a body of water, and preferably a place where you're allowed a small campfire.

### Supplies:

Candles, one for each participant plus one more, and a candleholder for each. Any color candles are fine, but red or pink

are best since they are in tune with loving, romantic vibrations.

Jasmine oil, rose oil, or patchouli oil (use pure, natural essential oils, not synthetics)

Small pieces of notepaper and pens with blue ink, enough for everyone to have a pen and several sheets of paper

Two cups, filled halfway with water

Two wands

A bell

### Pre-Ritual Preparations:

Dress in clothing that makes you feel sensual or good-looking. Shades of white, pink, red, or green are especially suitable. Light a small campfire if allowed. If not, place the additional candle in the center of the ritual space. In a circle surrounding it, place the candleholders. Beside the campfire or the center candle, place the two cups, the two wands, the bell, the notepaper, the pens, and the essential oil. Give one candle to each participant, and then select a person to lead the ritual. You will also need three additional volunteers to aid in the summoning of powers that takes place near the beginning of the ritual.

### The Ritual:

Have everyone stand in a circle, then have the person chosen as ritual leader walk around the circle ringing the bell. As they do so, participants should focus on the ringing sound of the bell, envisioning the space clearing of any negativity. The ritual leader should then make a second pass around the circle ringing the bell, this time with the intent of infusing the area with a positive vibration. Ritual participants can help with this process by conjuring up in their hearts a happy, loving feeling and projecting this outward, into the ritual space.

Next, the ritual leader and the three preselected volunteers should each pick up a cup or a wand, coming to the center of the circle where the other participants can see what is going on. The wands are raised high in the air, and the ritual participants focus on drawing down into the wands an active, assertive, masculine energy. If desired, specific deities or god-forms such as Cernunnos, Pan, the Horned God, or Belenos might be called at this point, directly invited to enter the circle through the points of the two wands held high. The two people with the wands then touch the wands together, forming an X and then switching their positions so that the wand that was in back is now in front, forming an X again. They say:

*Scepter to scepter, we welcome the energies of the Great God,*
*the active principle, the seed, the Animus!*
*Enter here now! Join us here now!*

Next, the two people holding the cups take center stage. The cups are raised high in the air and the ritualists concentrate on drawing down into the cups a more passive, nurturing, feminine energy. If desired, specific deities or godforms such as Anu, Brighid, Flora, Freya, or the Maiden Goddess might be summoned now—just ask them to enter the ritual space by first entering the water in the two cups.

The two people holding the cups then take turns pouring a bit of water into the other person's cup. They say:

*Cup to cup, we welcome the energies of the Great Goddess,*
*the subtle principle, the nurturer, the womb, the Anima!*
*Enter here now! Join us here now!*

Next, the two people with the wands should come forward and plunge the wands into the cups, one in each. One wand is moved in a clockwise motion while the other is moved in a counterclockwise motion, causing the water in the cups to swirl. The ritual leader and the three volunteers say in unison:

*Scepter to cup, we acknowledge the sacredness of all creation;*
*we welcome love and light in all its multiple and many forms!*

The volunteers then return to their original places in the circle.

Next, the ritual leader picks up the essential oil and makes his or her way around the circle, anointing the participants on palms, wrists, chest, and forehead. As this is done, they should envision the loving vibration of the oil seeping into the body of the anointed, filling them with glowing beauty and causing them to radiate with love. The ritual leader can enhance the effects of the oil by adding to the mix their own power. A feeling of love is conjured in the heart, and when the emotion is at its height, it's directed into the body of the participant through a straightforward application of visualization, will, and intention. As the ritual leader anoints the participants and fills each one with a feeling of radiating love and beauty, they say to each person:

*You are love. You are beautiful, and you are loved. You are love.*

Once everyone has been anointed, the final person in the circle should anoint the ritual leader. Then, the ritual leader can return the oil to its place near the center candle or campfire. The ritual leader circles the center candle or campfire three times, envisioning the loving energy that is now swirling around the space growing brighter, more powerful, and magnified. He or she then stops, holding his or her hands (safely!) above the flame, saying:

*By Great Beal's Fire, we empower our desire with the power of creation, with the power to inspire! By the powers here that be, we manifest all that we see!*

*Our light draws love and our love draws light!*
*We'll get just what we will tonight!*

The ritual leader then gently taps one of the participants, signaling them to go to the center of the circle where the center candle or campfire is burning brightly. That participant then carefully lights their own candle from the central fire, turning to face the circle and remaining in place. The participant then focuses their mind and emotions on their personal creative goals and/or on their wishes for love and romance. The other participants, including the ritual leader who has taken up a place in the circle, observe the ritualist standing in the center. The participants notice admirable, appealing, or attractive traits about the person, shouting them out as inspiration comes. For example, participants might say complimentary or supportive things such as "You have beautiful eyes and legs" or "You are worthy of love" or "You are beautiful inside and out." Just make sure the statements are coming from a place of compassion and authenticity. Most people can see right through empty flattery, and there's magick at hand, after all, so keep it real and keep it genuine.

At the ritual leader's signal, the participants then hold their hands out, open palms toward the ritualist who stands holding their candle at the center of the circle. The participants conjure a feeling of love in their hearts and minds, letting it radiate throughout the body then out through the hands and directly into the ritualist at the center. If any of the ritualists are new to the concept and practice of directing energy, visualization can be a big help. Imagine the energy you're directing as a glowing, tinted light, and charge that light with as much emotion as you can muster.

Once the participants have filled the center ritualist with this extra bit of "love power," that person then places their candle in one of the candleholders at the center and returns to their place in the circle. A new ritualist then takes their place near the center candle or campfire, lighting their own candle from that central flame and repeating the process of visualizing one's personal creative goals or romantic wishes, receiving the accolades and compliments of the crowd, receiving the loving energy from the crowd, placing their candle in one of the holders, then returning to the circle so that another ritualist can then have their turn at the center. Repeat the whole process with every participant, including the ritual leader.

Once everyone has finished at the fire, all participants should be in a circle, hands joined. A feeling of love is sent around the circle, projected from hand to hand, beginning and ending with the ritual leader. If you like, you can send the loving energy around the circle with a kiss rather than with holding hands—just pass a kiss around the circle from cheek to cheek, or if you are more adventurous, from lips to lips.

Once the loving energy has been raised satisfactorily, it's time for the next step. At the ritual leader's signal, everyone holds their hands toward the central fire, palms open, again projecting that loving energy, this time sending it into the flames. As this is happening, the ritual leader says, sending with the words a final boost of loving energy and magickal intention:

> *By love, by fire, by you, by me, by God, by Goddess,*
> *what we will, it will be!*

The heart of the ritual now complete, spend some time socializing with your ritual mates, talking openly about your romantic feelings and wishes and sharing creative ideas and aspirations. Use the notepaper and pens at the center of the circle to write short notes for one another, perhaps offering compliments and/or invitations for romantic adventure. The candles and/or campfire can be extinguished now, or if you are hanging around for a while, you can let them burn out on their own. Expect love and creativity to noticeably flourish in the lives of all participants, beginning immediately upon conclusion of the ritual and continuing for as long as several weeks or more, depending on the strength of the ritual and the effort of the participant in making the most of the ritual's effects.

# Quick Beltane Vigor and Youth Mini-Ritual for Groups, Partners, or Solitaries

Here's a Beltane ritual you can do when you have only moments to spare. It will quickly put you in touch with Beltane's fertile, creative energy flow, infusing you with fresh vigor and renewing youthful abilities of self-healing and regeneration. This ritual can be performed solo, with a partner, or with as many friends as you can gather. It will take only a few minutes from start to finish.

## Purpose:

The purpose of this ritual is to renew youth and restore vigor by attuning to Beltane's energetic current of fertility, growth, and creation.

## Setting:

Daytime, preferably early morning when the ground is still wet with dew, in an outdoor location where the ground is soft and covered with vegetation.

## Supplies:

None

## Pre-Ritual Preparations:

Wear something you won't mind rolling around on the ground in!

## The Ritual:

Sit or lay on the ground, making as much contact between your skin and the earth as is comfortable. Stroke the vegetation with your hands, petting the leaves or blades of grass slowly and gently. Let the vegetation slide between your fingers, and sense the energies of the plants flowing into you as you do so. If there is dew on the ground, collect it on your palms and rub the dew into your face, anointing cheeks, lips, forehead, chin, and the area surrounding your eyes. Rub some dew into your hands, as well. If you're starting too late in the day for dew, substitute with a bit of vegetation, selecting an especially healthy-looking leaf or flower with which to stroke your face and hands. Whether it's dew or vegetation, envision a vigorous, thriving energy flowing into your body as you touch it to your skin. Say:

*Like the plants of the earth, like the fresh morning dew,*
*I am healthy and growing, youthful and new!*

The ritual is now complete. Expect a feeling of renewal and energy to set in soon after. Effects should last throughout the growing season, helping to improve and sustain health, increase energy levels, and strengthen one's sense of youth and vigor.

CORRESPONDENCES
FOR
BELTANE

...ance, growth, passion, love, union, cooperation, fertility, fairy...

...tection, purification, manifestation, handfastings, building sacred...

...visiting sacred wells, giving offerings, working with faeries, vital...

...lking the boundaries of one's property, protecting plants, divin...

...nimals, people, and possessions astronomical midpoint, and sun...

...the spring equinox and summer solstice: Sun at 15 degrees of...

...n the northern hemisphere, Sun at 15 degrees of Scorpio in...

...uthern hemisphere. Female: Maiden Goddess, Mother Godde...

...Earth Goddess, water plants or animals, the Lover preparin...

...with her beloved Flora, Danu, Freyja, Maia, Shasti, Pros...

...Chin-hua fu-jen, Venus, Diana, Artemis, Aphrodite, Astart...

...ona, Rauni, Sarasvati, Horae, Pan, Cernunnos, Beal, Bala...

...Pluto Wotan, Odin, Oak King, Apollo, Ra, Mugwort Lu...

...ertility, protection, divination, communication, with spirits ener...

...purification, joy, love, prophetic dreams, renewal energy, vitality...

...wealth, fairy magick, luck success, strength Rose, Frankincens...

...smine, Lemon, Pine, Mint visiting sacred wells, giving offer...

...faeries, abundance, growth, passion, love, union, cooperation, fertil...

...tection, purification, manifestation, handfastings, building sacred...

## Spiritual Focus and Keywords

Abundance

creation

fertility

growth

love

psychic ability

purification

sexuality

union

## Magickal Focus

Abundance

cooperation

fertility

growth

love

manifestation

passion

protection
purification
union

## Suggested Workings
Building sacred fires
giving offerings
handfastings
protecting plants, animals, people, and possessions
visiting sacred wells
walking the boundaries of one's property
working with faeries

## Astrological Timing and Associated Planets
Astronomical midpoint between the Spring Equinox and Summer Solstice; Sun at 15 degrees of Taurus in the Northern Hemisphere, Sun at 15 degrees of Scorpio in the Southern Hemisphere. Some Pagans celebrate Beltane on the astronomical date, while others stick to May 1 out of tradition. Still others wait for visible clues in nature. When the hawthorn blossoms, it's a signal that Beltane has officially arrived.

## Archetypes
FEMALE
Earth Goddess

goddesses associated with water, plants, or animals
the Lover preparing to lie with her Beloved
Maiden Goddess
Mother Goddess

MALE
Dying and resurrecting gods
gods associated with fire, plants, or animals
Green Man
Horned God
Lord of the wild wood
the lusty young god getting ready to fertilize the goddess
    earth with his seed
Sun gods

### *Deities and Heroes*
GODDESSES
Aphrodite (Greek)
Artemis (Greek)
Astarte (Greek)
Bona Dea (Roman)
Chin-hua-fu-jen (Chinese)
Danu (Irish)
Diana (Roman)
Flora (Roman)
Freya (Norse)

Horae (Greek)

Maia (Greek)

Prosperina (Roman)

Rauni (Finnish)

Sarasvati (Hindu)

Venus (Roman)

### Gods
Apollo (Greek)

Baldur (Norse)

Beal, Bel, or Belenos (Celtic)

Cernunnos (Celtic)

Chung K'uei (Chinese)

Horned God (Celtic)

Odin (Norse)

Pan (Greek)

Pluto (Greek)

Ra (Egyptian)

Wotan (Germanic)

## *Colors*

*Brown:* Animals, earth energies, family, protection, wealth

*Green:* Abundance, fertility, growth, health, life, prosperity, vegetation, wealth

*Pink:* Beauty, cooperation, contentment, friendship, love, nurture, romance

*White:* Lunar energies, purity, power, protection

*Yellow:* Communication, dream work, happiness, solar
  energies

## Herbs

*Lemon:* Energy, joy, love, prophetic dreams, purification

*Mint:* Energy, healing, love, prosperity, protection, purification,
  renewal, vitality

*Mugwort:* Communication with spirits, divination, fertility,
  lust, protection

*Woodruff:* Protection, victory, wealth

## Trees

*Birch:* Fertility, protection, purification

*Hawthorn:* Faery magick, fertility, defense, happiness, luck,
  protection

*Oak:* Courage, energy, fertility, luck, magick, protection,
  security, strength

*Pine:* Abundance, energy, fertility, prosperity, purification

*Willow:* Communication with spirits, healing, love, lunar
  energies, prophetic dreams, protection

## Flowers

*Daisy:* Attraction, elf and faery magic, love, youth

*Ivy:* Divination, friendship, love, luck, marriage, rebirth,
  security

*Lily of the Valley:* Desire, healing, love, peace, protection
*Rose:* Blessings, clairvoyance, friendship, love, protection
*Violet:* Calming, fertility, love, protection, prophetic dreams

## Crystals and Stones
*Bloodstone:* Abundance, courage, healing, love, passion, wealth
*Emerald:* Luck, love, prosperity, protection, wealth
*Rose quartz:* Friendship, love, nurture, union

## Metals
*Copper:* Energy, love, prosperity, well-being
*Gold:* Health, love, magick, protection, strength,
    solar energies, success, wealth
*Silver:* Love, lunar energies, magick, prophetic dreams,
    psychic ability

## Animals, Totems, and Mythical Creatures
*Bees:* Energy, karma, romance, prosperity
*Cow:* Abundance, fertility, nurture, wealth
*Dove:* Fertility, happiness, life, peace, rebirth
*Frog:* Abundance, beginnings, fertility, luck, transformation
*Rabbit:* Abundance, fertility, intuition, love

### Scents for Oils, Incense, Potpourri, or Just Floating in the Air

Frankincense

jasmine

lemon

mint

pine

rose

woodruff

ylang-ylang

### Tarot Keys

The Emperor

the Empress

the High Priestess

the Magician

### Symbols and Tools

Flowers (symbolizing fertility, love, and joy)

maypole (symbolizing fertility and the male phallus)

the priapic (pinecone-tipped) wand (symbolizing fertility and
    sexuality)

*Foods*

Honey

light cakes

*Drinks*

Lemonade

May Wine made with white wine, lemon slices,
    and woodruff milk

*Activities and Traditions of Practice*

Bringing in the May (collecting foliage the night before and
    placing it in and on the home in time for the May Day
    sunrise)

decorating a May Bush

distributing May baskets

divination

feasting

fertility magick

handfastings and other romantic partnerships

lighting bonfires

making offerings to deities, ancestors, and faeries

Maypole dancing

nature walks

purification ceremonies

protection rituals

sacred sex

singing

visiting wells

## Acts of Service

Beautifying a neighbor's living quarters with fresh flowers
    and herbs

planting a tree

rehabilitating the banks of a stream

removing litter from an outdoor area

working on a community garden

## Alternative Names for Beltane in Other Pagan Traditions

Cetsamhain (Celtic, meaning Opposite Samhain)

Lá Bealtaine (Celtic, meaning Day of Beltane)

May Day (widespread usage)

Walpurgisnacht (Germanic, meaning Walpurgis Night)

## Holidays or Traditions Occurring
## During Beltane in the Northern Hemisphere

RELIGIOUS

Rowan Witch Day (Finnish, May 1)

Sacred Thorn Tree Day (Irish, May 4)

Festival of Shashti (Hindu, May 12)

SECULAR

Earth Day (April 22)

Walpurgis Night (Germanic, April 30)

May Day (European, May 1)

Mother's Day (most of Europe, North America, and many
other countries around the world celebrate sometime in
May)

## *Holidays or Traditions Occurring During Beltane in the Southern Hemisphere*

RELIGIOUS

All Soul's Day (Christian Catholic, some Protestant denominations)

Diwali (Hindu)

Hollantide (Welsh)

Martinmass (Christian Catholic)

SECULAR

Guy Fawkes Day (UK)

Halloween

Recreation Day (northern Tasmania)

# FURTHER READING

## Books

Cunningham, Scott. *Living Wicca: A Further Guide for the Solitary Practioner.* St. Paul, MN: Llewellyn Worldwide, 1993.

Hutton, Ronald. *The Stations of the Sun: A History of the Ritual Year in Britain.* New York: Oxford University Press, 1996.

*Llewellyn's 2011–2012 Sabbats Almanac.* Woodbury, MN: Llewellyn Worldwide, 2012.

*Llewellyn's 2012–2013 Sabbats Almanac.* Woodbury, MN: Llewellyn Worldwide, 2012.

*Llewellyn's 2013–2014 Sabbats Almanac.* Woodbury, MN: Llewellyn Worldwide, 2013.

MacLeod, Sharon Paice. *Celtic Myth and Religion: A Study of Traditional Belief, with Newly Translated Prayers, Poems, and Songs.* Jefferson, NC: McFarland and Company, 2012.

Raedisch, Linda. *Night of the Witches: Folklore, Traditions, and Recipes for Celebrating Walpurgis Night.* Woodbury, MN: Llewellyn Worldwide, 2011.

Turcan, Robert. *The Gods of Ancient Rome: Religion in Everyday Life from Archaic to Imperial.* New York: Routledge, 2001.

## *Online*

Frazer, James George, Sir. *The Golden Bough.* New York: Macmillan, 1922; Bartleby.com, 2000. http://www.bartleby.com/196/.

Hyde, Douglas. *A Literary History of Ireland from Earliest Times to the Present Day.* London: 1906. Google EBooks, 2010. http://books.google.com/books/about/A_literary_history_of_Ireland_from_earli.html?id=x89MAAAAYAAJ.

Moore, A. W. *Folk-lore of the Isle of Man.* London: D. Nutt, 1891, Chapter VI, "Customs and Superstitions Connected with the Seasons." Sacred-texts.com, 2005. http://www.sacred-texts.com/neu/celt/fim/fim00.htm.

# BIBLIOGRAPHY

## Books

Associated Newspapers, Ltd. *The Complete Book of Fortune*. 1935. Reprint. New York: Crescent Books, 1990.

Balk, Antti P. *Saints and Sinners: An Account of Western Civilization*. London: Thelema Publications, 2008.

Ball, Ann. *Catholic Traditions in the Garden*. Huntington, IN: Our Sunday Visitor, 1998.

Bramshaw, Vikki. *Craft of the Wise: A Practical Guide to Paganism and Witchcraft*. Ropely, UK: Obooks, 2009.

Buckland, Raymond. *Buckland's Book of Saxon Witchcraft*. York Beach: Weiser, 2005.

Cockrell, Dale. *Demons of Disorder: Early Blackface Minstrels and their World*. New York: Cambridge University Press, 1997.

Conway, D. J. *Moon Magick*. St. Paul, MN: Llewellyn Publication, 1995.

Coppens, Phillip. *Land of the Gods: How a Scottish Landscape was Sanctified to Become Arthur's "Camelot."* Amsterdam: Frontier Publishing, 2007.

Cunningham, Scott. *The Complete Book of Incense, Oils, and Brews*. St. Paul, MN: Llewellyn Publications, 1996.

Curran, Bob. *Walking with the Green Man: Father of the Forest, Spirit of Nature*. Franklin Lakes, NJ: New Page Books / The Career Press, 2007.

Doniger, Wendy, ed. *Merriam-Webster's Encyclopedia of World Religions*. Springfield, MA: Merriam-Webster, 1999.

Futrell, Alison. *Blood in the Arena: The Spectacle of Roman Power*. Austin, TX: University of Texas Press, 1997.

Graves, Robert. *The White Goddess: A Historical Grammar of Poetic Myth*. New York: Farrar, Straus, and Giroux, 2013. First published in 1948 by Creative Age Press.

Green, Mandy. *Milton's Ovidian Eve*. Surrey: Ashgate Publishing Limited, 2009.

Hutton, Ronald. *The Stations of the Sun: A History of the Ritual Year in Britain*. New York: Oxford University Press, 1996.

Jordan, Michael. *Dictionary of Gods and Goddesses, Second Edition*. New York: Facts on File, 2004.

Knight, Stephen, ed. *Robin Hood: An Anthology of Scholarship and Criticism*. Suffolk: D. S. Brewer, 1999.

Koch, John T., ed. *Celtic Culture: A Historical Encyclopedia*. Santa Barbara, CA: ABC-CLIO, 2006.

Littleton, C. Scott, ed. *Gods, Goddesses, and Mythology, Volume 4*. Tarrytown, NY: Marshall Cavendish, 2010.

MacCulloch, J. A. *The Religion of the Ancient Celts*. Electronic book. Boston: Mobile Reference, 2010.

MacLeod, Sharon Paice. *Celtic Myth and Religion: A Study of Traditional Belief, with Newly Translated Prayers, Poems, and Songs*. Jefferson, NC: McFarland and Company, 2012.

Matthews, John. *The Quest for the Green Man*. Wheaton, IL: Quest Books, 2001.

Monaghan, Patricia. *The Encyclopedia of Celtic Mythology and Folklore*. New York: Facts on File, 2004.

Mountain, Harry. *The Celtic Encyclopedia, Volume 2*. Boca Raton, FL: Universal Publishers, 1998.

*National Geographic Essential Visual History of World Mythology*. Des Moines, IA: National Geographic Books, 2008.

Newlands, Carole E. *Playing with Time: Ovid and the Fasti*. Ithaca, NY: Cornell University Press, 1995.

Otnes, Cele C., and Tina M. Lowry, eds. *Contemporary Consumption Rituals: A Research Anthology.* Mahwah, NJ: Lawrence Erlbaum Associates, 2004.

Rich, Vivian A. *Cursing the Basil: And Other Folklore of the Garden.* Victoria, BC: Horsdal and Schubart Publishers, 1998.

Thompson, Francis. *The Supernatural Highlands.* London: Robert Hale and Company, 1976.

Turcan, Robert. *The Gods of Ancient Rome: Religion in Everyday Life from Archaic to Imperial.* New York: Routledge, 2001.

Watts, D. C. *Dictionary of Plant Lore.* Burlington, MA: Elsevier, 2007.

Woodard, Roger D. *Myth, Ritual, and the Warrior in Roman and Indo-European Antiquity.* New York: Cambridge University Press, 2013.

## Online

Asatru Alliance. "Runic Era Calendar." Accessed December 20, 2013. http://www.asatru.org/holidays.php.

Austin, C. "Beltaine." Accessed December 20, 2013. http://www.irishculturalsociety.org/essaysandmisc/beltaine.html.

Beltane at Thornborough. Accessed December 20, 2013. http://www.celebratebeltane.co.uk/.

Beltane Fire Society. "Beltane Audience Experience." Accessed December 20, 2013. http://beltanefiresociety
.wordpress.com/beltane-audience-experience/.

Beltania.org. "May 8–11, 2014: Feeding the Fires. Accessed December 20, 2013. http:/www.beltania.org.

Blue Ridge Beltane. Accessed December 20, 2013.
http://blueridgebeltane.org/.

Bonwick, James. *Irish Druids and Old Irish Religions*. London: Griffith, Farran, 1894; Sacred-Texts.com, 2002. Accessed December 20, 2013. http://www.sacred-texts.com/pag
/idr/idr00.htm.

Burdick, Lewis Dayton. *Magic and Husbandry: The Folk-lore of Agriculture.* Binghamton, NY: Otseningo Publishing, 1905; Google EBooks, 2005. http://books.google.
com/books?id=M0LOO7kQBBQC&lpg=PA132&ots=_
hfFfgIxRF&dq=Magic%20and%20Husbandry%3A%20
The%20Folklore%20of%20Agriculture&pg=PR3#v
=onepage&q=Magic%20and%20Husbandry:%20The%20
Folklore%20of%20Agriculture&f=false.

Burns, David. *The May Queen: A Thespis*. London: Simpkin, Marshall and Co., 1894; Google EBooks, 2010. http://
books.google.com/books?id=c7NMAAAAYAAJ&pg=PP1
#v=onepage&q&f=false.

Clogerheritage.com. "May Day in the West of Ireland." Accessed January 20, 2014. http://www.clogherheritage
.com/stories3.html.

"Council Faces Clean-up Bill after Maybush Fires." *Wicklow People*, May 5, 2005. http://www.independent.ie/regionals/wicklowpeople/news/council-faces-cleanup-bill-after-maybush-fires-27830655.html.

CR FAQ. "What do you do for Bealtaine?" Accessed January 20, 2014. http://www.paganachd.com/faq/ritual.html#bealtaine.

Cutting, Jennifer. Transcript of "Bringing in the May." Journeys and Crossings, Library of Congress. Accessed December 20, 2013. http://www.loc.gov/rr/program/journey/mayday-transcript.html.

Daniels, Cora Linn, and Charles McClellan Stevans, PhD, eds. *Encyclopedia of Superstitions, Folklore, and the Occult Sciences of the World, Volume III.* Chicago, IL: 1903; Google EBooks, 2008. http://books.google.com/books?id=ns0gK0efOvYC&pg=PA1191#v=onepage&q&f=false.

Davis, Joseph Barnard, and John Thurnam. *Crania Britannica.* London: 1865; Google EBooks, 2012. http://books.google.com.books?id=Df0wAQAAMAAJ&dq=Crania%20Britannica&pg=PP7#v=onepage&q=Crania%20Britannica&f=false.

Diprose, Ted. "Hobbyhorse." Accessed December 20, 2013. http://www.merciangathering.com/silverwheel/hobbyhorse.htm.

Druid of Fisher Street, The. "ADF Beltane 2011." Accessed December 20, 2013. http://thedruidoffisherst.blogspot.com/2011/05/adf-beltane-2011.html.

*Encyclopedia Britannica.* "Flora." Accessed December 20, 2013. http://www.britannica.com/EBchecked/topic/210597/Flora.

*Encyclopedia Britannica.* "Morris dance." Accessed January 20, 2014. http://www.britannica.com/EBchecked/topic/392943/Morris-dance.

*Encyclopedia Britannica.* "Mumming Play." Accessed January 20, 2014. http://www.britannica.com/EBchecked/topic/397332/mumming-play.

Fleming, Thomas. "Stone Secrets of the First Americans." Accessed December 20, 2013. http://www.ensignmessage.com/stonesecrets.html.

Flippo, Hyde. "German Holidays and Customs in May." Accessed December 20, 2013. http://german.about.com/od/holidaysfolkcustoms/a/mai.htm.

Fosbroke, Thomas Dudley. *Encyclopedia of Antiquities and Elements of Archeaology, Classical and Medieval, Volume 2.* London: Nattali, 1825; Google EBooks, 2010. http://books.google.com/books?id=Gcv4WxCSK0gC&dq=inauthor%3A%22Thomas%20Dudley%20Fosbroke%22&pg=PA483#v=onepage&q&f=false.

Fowler, William Warde. *The Roman Festivals of the Period of the Republic.* London: Macmillan, 1899; Google EBooks, 2005. http://books.google.com/books?id=_2w01mQEOBAC& pg=PR3&source=gbs_selected_pages&cad=3#v=onepag e&q&f=false.

Frazer, James George, Sir. *The Golden Bough.* New York: Macmillan, 1922; Bartleby.com, 2000. http://www.bartleby .com/196/.

French Moments. "May Day in France." Accessed December 20, 2013. http://www.frenchmoments.eu/may-day-in -france-la-fete-du-travail/.

Harman, Daniel P. "Public Festivals of Rome." *Principat, Volume 16, part 2.* Edited by Wolfgang Haase 2. Berlin: Walter de Gruyter, 1978. Google EBooks.

Helsinki.fi. "Vappu: Celebrating Spring and Student Life!" (blog). April 30, 2013. http://blogs.helsinki.fi/welcome-touh/2013/04/30/vappu-celebrating-spring-and-student -life/.

Heritage Newfoundland. "The May Bush in Newfoundland." Accessed December 20, 2013. http://www.heritage.nf.ca /society/custom_may_bush.html.

Hyde, Douglas. *A Literary History of Ireland from Earliest Times to the Present Day.* London: 1906. Reprint, Google EBooks, 2010. http://books.google.com/books?id=x89MAAAAYA AJ&pg=PR5#v=onepage&q&f=false.

In the Heart of the Beast Puppet and Mask Theatre. "May-Day." Accessed December 20, 2013. http://hobt.org /mayday/.

*Internet Book of Shadows*. "Beltane Ritual." Shadow Weaver Grove ADF. 1990. Accessed December 20, 2013. http://www.sacred-texts.com/bos/bos630.htm.

Kondratiev, Alexei. "Samhain: Season of Death and Renewal." Accessed December 20, 2013. http://www.imbas.org /articles/samhain.html.

Kubilius, Kerry. "Estonia's Holidays." Accessed December 20, 2013. http://goeasteurope.about.com/od /estoniatravel/a/Estonia-Holidays.htm.

Lambert, Victoria. "Beltane: Britain's Ancient Festival Is Making a Comeback." *The Telegraph*, April 27, 2012. Accessed December 20, 2013. http://www.telegraph.co.uk/life-style/9230904/Beltane-Britains-ancient-festival-is-making -a-comeback.html.

Library Ireland. "Beltane." Accessed December 20, 2013. http://www.libraryireland.com/Druids/Beltane.php.

Lyons, Reneé Critcher. *The Revival of Banned Dances: A World-wide Study*. Jefferson, NC: McFarland and Company, 2012.

Magickal Cat, The. "Herbal Grimoire." Accessed December 20, 2013. http://www.themagickalcat.com/Articles .asp?ID=242.

"May-Day Basket Custom Related." *Prescott Evening Courier*. April 24, 1952. Accessed December 20, 2013. http://news .google.com/newspapers?nid=897&dat=19520424&id=Eb JaAAAAIBAJ&sjid=CFADAAAAIBAJ&pg=5913,4928686.

Maypoledance.com. "All About Maypole Dancing." Accessed December 20, 2013. http://www.maypoledance.com /maypole.html.

McNeill, Maggie. "Floralia." Accessed December 20, 2013. http://maggiemcneill.wordpress.com/2012/05/03/floralia/.

Moonstone, Rowan. "Beltane: Its History and Modern Celebration in Wicca in America." *Internet Book of Shadows*. Sacred-Texts, 1990. Accessed January 20, 2014. http://www.sacred-texts.com/bos/bos032.htm.

Moore, A. W. *Folk-lore of the Isle of Man*. London: D. Nutt, 1891; Sacred-Texts, 2005. Accessed December 20, 2013. http://www.sacred-texts.com/neu/celt/fim/fim00.htm.

Moriarty, Colm. "Mayday and the Celtic festival of Bealtaine." Irish Archeology, May 1, 2011. Accessed December 20, 2013. http://irisharchaeology.ie/2011/05/mayday-and -bealtaine/.

My Czech Republic. "May First, the Time of Love." Accessed January 20, 2013. http://www.myczechrepublic.com /czech_culture/czech_holidays/may.html.

National Museum of Ireland. "Bonfires and Dancing." Accessed December 20, 2013. http://www.museum.ie/en/list/topic-may-day.aspx?article=8eba7384-49e2-4ba0-8613-1cfa8f153ed5.

Nemeton the Sacred Grove. "Belenos." Accessed December 20, 2013. http://www.celtnet.org.uk/gods_b/belenos.html.

Nottinghamshire County Council. "Robin Hood." Accessed December 20, 2013. http://www.nottinghamshire.gov.uk/enjoying/countryside/countryparks/sherwood/sherwoodforesthistory/robinhoodhistory/.

*New World Encyclopedia.* "Beltane." Accessed January 20, 2014. http://www.newworldencyclopedia.org/entry/Beltane.

Owen, James. "Druids Committed Human Sacrifice, Cannibalism?" *National Geographic News* March 20, 2009. Accessed January 20, 2013. http://news.nationalgeographic.com/news/2009/03/090320-druids-sacrifice-cannibalism.html.

Padstow Museum. "The Mystery of Mayday." Accessed December 20, 2013. http://home.freeuk.com/padstowmuseum/Mayday_Mystery.htm.

Pagan Lore. Artisson, Robin. "The Differences in Traditional Witchcraft and Neo-Pagan Witchcraft, or Wicca." Last modified 2001, accessed December 20, 2013. http://www.paganlore.com/witchcraft_vs_wicca.aspx.

Planet Vermont. Angel, Paul Tudor. "The Mysterious Mega-
liths of New England." Accessed December 20, 2013.
http://planetvermont.com/pvq/v9n1/megaliths.html.

Project Britain. "May Day." Accessed December 20, 2013.
http://resources.woodlands-junior.kent.sch.uk/customs
/questions/mayday.htm.

Sanders, M. "Yorkshire's Stonehenge: The Thornborough
Henges." Accessed December 20, 2013. http://www
.prehistory.yas.org.uk/content/thornborough.html.

Sanford, D. K. *The Popular Encyclopedia, Volume 6.* London,
Blackie & Son, 1841; Google EBooks, 2008. http://books
.google.com/books?id=9kjCqERYQIcC&pg=PR5#v=one
page&q&f=false.

Seymour, William Wood. *The Cross in Tradition, History,
and Art.* New York: Putnam, 1898; Google EBooks, 2008.
http://books.google.com/books?id=rhMtAAAAYAAJ&l
pg=PA481&ots=0hhAuhDHaQ&dq=The%20Cross%20
in%20Tradition%2C%20History%2C%20and%20Art%20
80&pg=PP9#v=onepage&q=The%20Cross%20in%20
Tradition,%20History,%20and%20Art%2080&f=false.

Shadow Weaver Grove ADF. "Beltane Ritual." *Internet Book of
Shadows.* Sacred-texts, 1990. Accessed December 20, 2013.
http://www.sacred-texts.com/bos/bos630.htm.

Sieg, George. "Heathen May Celebration." *Examiner.com*, May 4, 2010. Accessed December 20, 2013. http://www .examiner.com/article/heathen-may-celebration.

Smith, William, and Charles Anthon, eds. *A Dictionary of Greek and Roman Antiquities.* London: J. Murray, 1901; Google EBooks, 2009. http://books.google.com/ books?id=Cu89AAAAYAAJ&dq=A%20Dictionary%20 of%20Greek%20and%20Roman%20Antiquities&pg=PA86 7#v=snippet&q=floralia&f=false.

Spoutwood Farm. "The 22nd Annual May Day Fairie Festival." Accessed December 20, 2013. http://www .spoutwood.org/fairie-festival/about.

Stoll, Heinrich Wilhelm. *Handbook of the Religion and Mythology of the Greeks, with a Short Account of the Religious System of the Romans.* Translated by R. B. Paul. London: Francis and John Rivington, 1852; Google EBooks, 2006. http://books.google.com/books?id=UWoBAAAAQAAJ &dq=Handbook%20of%20the%20Religion%20and%20 Mythology%20of%20the%20Greeks%2C%20with%20 a%20Short%20Account%20of%20the%20Religious%20 System%20of%20the%20Romans&pg=PR1#v=onepage& q&f=false.

Theoi Greek Mythology. "Khloris." Accessed December 20, 2013. http://www.theoi.com/Nymphe/NympheKhloris .html.

Traditionalwitch.net. "Beltane." June 19, 2010. Accessed December 20, 2013. http://www.traditionalwitch.net/_
/esoterica/festivals-sabbats/beltane-r32.

Turtle Hill Events. "Beltane Gathering, The." Accessed December 20, 2013. http://www.turtlehillevents.org
/beltane/.

University of Chicago. "Floralia." Accessed January 20, 2014. http://penelope.uchicago.edu/~grout/encyclopaedia
_romana/calendar/floralia.html.

Williams, Margaret. "Beltane Essay 1." Witchvox, May 4, 1999. Accessed January 20, 2014. http://www.witchvox
.com/va/dt_va.html?a=usxx&c=holidays&id=2343.

# ENDNOTES

1. This may have been a type of fungus known as fly agaric, a red and white capped mushroom with potent psychoactive properties and high levels of toxicity.

2. Vetches are a small flowering plant used to feed farm animals.

3. Lupins are a type of legume with colorful yellow pods.

4. Cowslip is the common name for *Primula veris*, a flowering plant related to the primrose that produces bright yellow blossoms in the spring.

5. One commonly misunderstood aspect of historic mummers plays and Morris dancing that bears mentioning stems from the performers' early use of black makeup to completely mask the face. The makeup was originally used not as an allusion to race, but rather, it was intended to symbolize the idea of the "Other," the darkness, the potential gruesomeness and cruelty of the night. As the act of blackening the face lost its original symbolism and became racially offensive, this aspect of the masquerade was largely dropped in Morris dancing and mummers plays alike. For more information, see *Demons of Disorder: Early Blackface Minstrels and Their World* by Dale Cockrell (New York: Cambridge University Press, 1997), 50–54.

# INDEX

bull, 17, 19

burning of the witches, 39

**F**

## About the Author

**Melanie Marquis** is a lifelong practitioner of magick, founder of the United Witches global coven, and organizer of Denver Pagans. She is a writer who has written for the American Tarot Association, Llewellyn's almanacs and datebooks, and national and international Pagan publications including *Circle* and *Pentacle* magazines. She resides in Colorado. Visit her online at www.melaniemarquis.com.

## Other Books by This Author

Lughnasadh

A Witch's World of Magick

The Witch's Bag of Tricks

Witchy Mama

Modern Spellcaster's Tarot